Further praise for *Sales Enablement:*

"Tamara and Byron could have titled this book *'Outside/In'*
Sales Enablement! They put the focus on building your sales
enablement strategy where it should be – on your customer.
A must-read, whether you're a sales enablement pro or just
getting started!"

—JIM NINIVAGGI, Sales Enablement Leader,
Chief Readiness Officer

"Sales enablement is definitely a fast-growing discipline and
the information inside this rich, yet easy to understand book
will allow you to execute on this discipline so easily and
effortlessly."

—BERNADETTE MCCLELLAND, CEO
3 Red Folders, Sales and Leadership Expert

"A book that demystifies sales enablement and provides a
seminal clarity model, which serves as a valuable roadmap
for organizations at all levels of their sales enablement
journey."

—DR. HOWARD DOVER, Director,
Center for Professional Sales at UT Dallas

SALES ENABLEMENT

SALES ENABLEMENT

*A Master Framework to Engage,
Equip, and Empower
A World-Class Sales Force*

BYRON MATTHEWS | TAMARA SCHENK

WILEY

Published by John Wiley & Sons, Inc., Hoboken, New Jersey.
Published simultaneously in Canada.

For general information on our other products and services or for technical support, please contact our Customer Care Department within the United States at (800) 762–2974, outside the United States at (317) 572–3993 or fax (317) 572–4002.

Wiley publishes in a variety of print and electronic formats and by print-on-demand. Some material included with standard print versions of this book may not be included in e-books or in print-on-demand. If this book refers to media such as a CD or DVD that is not included in the version you purchased, you may download this material at http://booksupport.wiley.com. For more information about Wiley products, visit www.wiley.com.

Library of Congress Cataloging-in-Publication Data

Names: Matthews, Byron, 1973- author. | Schenk, Tamara, 1967- author.
Title: Sales enablement : a master framework to engage, equip, and empower a world-class sales
    force / Byron Matthews, Tamara Schenk.
Description: Hoboken : Wiley, 2018. | Includes index. |
Identifiers: LCCN 2018005465 (print) | ISBN 9781119440277 (hardback)
Subjects: LCSH: Selling. | Leadership. | Customer relations. | Teams in the workplace. |
    BISAC: BUSINESS & ECONOMICS / Sales & Selling.
Classification: LCC HF5438.25 .M376 2018 (print) | DDC 658.8/102–dc23
LC record available at https://lccn.loc.gov/2018005465

ISBN 978-1-119-44027-7 (hbk)
ISBN 978-1-119-44030-7 (ebk)
ISBN 978-1-119-44029-1 (ebk)

Printed in the United States of America

10 9 8 7 6 5 4 3 2

Contents

Special Thanks from the Authors

From Tamara – The world of sales enablement as we discuss it in this book is a rather young discipline, so I would like to thank those individuals who were already working in the enablement space a couple of years ago when the first enablement communities were built. My special thanks go to Scott Santucci, the founder of The Sales Enablement Society. I worked with Scott when he was a Forrester analyst to successfully evolve sales enablement to a strategic function in my previous role as VP Global Sales Enablement at T-Systems. Also, to Christian Maurer, who is my go-to person when I need my concepts and frameworks deeply challenged. And of course, Joe Galvin, who hired me and coached me into my new analyst role. Regarding the birth of this much needed sales enablement book, many thanks to Byron Matthews for initiating the idea for co-authoring this book.

From Byron – Selling is my passion, and I cannot imagine a more gratifying career. For that, I have to thank Accenture, Aflac and Mercer for the great opportunities they gave me. These are incredible organizations, and my time there shaped who I am today. I would also like to thank all of the wonderful Miller

Heiman Group clients for sharing their passion for selling with us. You are a daily inspiration, and I am grateful for the opportunity to be part of your journey.

From both of us – Melissa Paulik, the book wouldn't exist without you, thanks so much for all the work you have done to structure our thoughts and ideas and to organize and integrate them into our central theme. Many thanks to Seleste Lunsford for her highly effective leadership, her ideas and advice; Paul Maxwell for his excellent editing work; the rest of the CSO Insights team, especially Jim Dickie and Barry Trailer for their support, ideas and advice; and last but not least, Robin Stasiak for her excellent project management.

Moving from sales enablement practitioner to analyst comes with a few challenges, not the least of which is the move from telling our own enablement stories to telling those of others. We would like to thank those sales enablement professionals and business leaders, including Christine Dorrion, Robert Racine, Jim Burns, Boris Kluck, Sam Trachtenberg, Ryan Toben, Kai Yu Hsuing and Thierry van Herwijnen, each of whom took the time to share the details of their stories with us as we worked through the examples in the book. Your efforts breathed life into the points we needed to make.

We'd also like to thank the many experts who took the time to provide their point of view and sage advice, including Jill Rowley, Social Selling Evangelist and Chief Growth Officer at Marketo; Jay Mitchell of Mereo; Erik Rentsch of Code SixFour; Sam Herring and Catie Bull of Intrepid and Treion Muller of TwentyEighty. As always, your perspectives and insights helped us strengthen our own.

Finally, we absolutely must thank the team at John Wiley & Sons for providing calm, patient guidance to the Miller Heiman Group book team, most of whom were going through the publishing process for the first time. Special thanks to Vicki Adang and Tessa Allen, who took us over the finish line and made sure we didn't lose our sanity in the process.

About the Authors

Byron Matthews is the Chief Executive Officer of Miller Heiman Group and leads their commitment to championing customer management excellence.

Over the past 23 years, Byron has consulted with and led sales organizations for several Fortune 500 companies. He has collaborated with industry leaders throughout the world at companies like Microsoft, AT&T, Samsung and Coca-Cola on the development of pipeline and revenue management solutions, implementation of sales methodologies, optimization of sales management processes and compensation plans and competency models linked to assessment and recruiting.

Byron's depth and breadth of prior experiences include serving as chief sales officer at Aflac, where he led over 30,000 sales professionals across multiple channels, and over five years at Mercer as global sales leader and global head of the Sales Performance Practice.

Byron received his MBA at the University of Chicago. Tamara Schenk, Research Director at CSO Insights, the research division of Miller Heiman Group, is focused on all things sales force enablement, sales managers, social selling and collaboration.

She has enjoyed more than 25 years of experience in sales, business development and consulting in different industries on an international level. Before becoming an analyst in a research director role in 2014, she had the pleasure of developing sales enablement from an idea to a program and a strategic function at T-Systems, a Deutsche Telekom company, where she led the global sales force enablement and transformation team.

Tamara is a member of The Sales Enablement Society, a regular contributor to Top Sales World and a featured writer for *Top Sales Magazine*. She graduated from the University of Hohenheim in Baden-Württemberg, Germany, with a Dipl. oec. in economics.

About Miller Heiman Group

MILLER HEIMAN GROUP empowers people across the entire organization to perform at peak potential by bringing game-changing insight to sales performance, customer experience and leadership and management. Backed by more than 150 years of experience and performance and built on several well-known brands such as Miller Heiman, AchieveGlobal, Huthwaite, Impact Learning Systems and Channel Enablers, we offer more sales- and customer service-based solutions than anyone in the industry. This allows companies to build and sustain successful, customer-focused organizations that drive profitable revenue and top-line growth on a global scale. To learn more, visit our website and follow us on LinkedIn, Twitter, Facebook, YouTube or Google+.

About CSO Insights

CSO INSIGHTS IS the independent research arm within Miller Heiman Group™ dedicated to improving the performance and productivity of complex B2B sales. The CSO Insights team of respected analysts provides sales leaders with the research, data, expertise and best practices required to build sustainable strategies for sales performance improvement. CSO Insights' annual sales effectiveness studies, along with its benchmarking capabilities, are industry standards for sales leaders seeking operational and behavioral insights into how to improve their sales performance and to gain holistic assessments of their selling and sales management efficacy. Annual research studies look at World-Class practices for sales and service optimization, sales enablement and sales operations.

Foreword

I FIRST MET Byron Matthews several years ago when my team and I were working to address a sales capability gap at LinkedIn. Over the course of our discussions, I immediately felt like Byron understood my world. What I appreciated most throughout the process, was that he was dead set on helping me solve my business problem rather than focusing on what the Miller Heiman Group had to offer. He worked with me in the same way we want our sales team to go-to-market – with the customers' needs at the forefront of every conversation.

Since then, Byron and I have stayed in touch, and I've watched the Miller Heiman Group expand their focus and continue to dive deeper into elevating the sales profession through top-notch sales enablement offerings. Needless to say, I was thrilled when they called and asked if I would be willing to write the forward to their book on sales enablement. While there are dozens of books on sales strategies, there are few on enabling sales teams that are designed for the sales enablement professional. This is the book I wish I had back when I started my career in sales enablement. More importantly, this isn't just a book for sales enablement teams – it's a book written for sales leaders, without whom sales enablement professionals fail, every time.

Over the years, I've worked with many sales leaders who think sales enablement is just about training or worse, event planning. They see their sales enablement partners as transactional support functions versus strategic business advisers. But you can't blame them because so many sales enablement teams focus so much of their effort on getting programs out the door that they fail to look at the system as a whole, working hand in hand with sales to solve real business problems. I know because I've made those mistakes, and I've experienced the failure that comes along with them. My take on the matter is simple. At the core, sales training by itself is ineffective almost 100% of the time. You need the right conditions to sustain newly learned skills, and you need an engaged sales leadership team to lead from the front and coach to create new habits over time. If you don't have this, you're wasting your time and your money.

If you are a sales leader looking to upskill your sales team, or you are a sales enablement professional trying to get a seat at the table, read on. The Miller Heiman Group approach to sales enablement is comprehensive and spot on, covering all of the elements of a true sales enablement discipline: content, training, technology, and one of my favorites, sales coaching. Every recommendation in the book is backed by research as well as by anecdotal evidence from sales leaders who have put these principles into practice. Perhaps most importantly, the book emphasizes the need for sales enablement teams to be insights-driven – using data to understand the return on your sales enablement investment, and better yet, how data can help sales leaders make better business decisions. You can't manage (or improve) what you can't measure, and the Miller Heiman Group gets it.

I know firsthand how hard the job of sales enablement is. For those of you in it with me, you have the potential to be one of, if not the most important partner to sales. But you can't get there if you don't prioritize building out each component of the sales enablement ecosystem. This comes with trade-offs you have to make and a vision you have to paint for your sales leadership team, backed by data and insights they can believe in.

This book gives you the guidance you need to make the shift from tactical support function to strategic partner, widely recognized for having a significant impact on sales performance and a key driver in transforming the most important part of the sales organization—the people.

Amy Borsetti
Senior Director, Global Sales Readiness
LinkedIn Corporation

PART

I

Introduction

SALES HAS NEVER been an easy profession, but our research shows that more salespeople than ever are struggling to make their numbers. Over the last five years, the percentage of salespeople making quota dropped by 10 points. The percentage of companies achieving revenue also dropped by nearly 4 points.

If you're in senior leadership, this performance decline can be incredibly frustrating. You've invested hundreds of thousands of dollars, if not millions, in CRM solutions and other technologies designed to make your salespeople more productive and effective. You've put considerable funding into developing training programs and sales collateral. You've honed your hiring practices and sought to attract top-notch talent with a proven track record in your industry. So why aren't you seeing a return on your investment?

Our answer is simple. Today's sales organizations are not keeping up with and adapting to the pace of change.

We all know how quickly things change. Just think about what you can do with the phone you use today as compared to the one you used just five years ago. From the technology itself to the apps that are available, the difference is night and day.

However, few of us take the time to think about the macro forces of change all around us and how they impact the profession we're in. We're not talking about the small things like the release of the latest iPhone. Or even more dramatic events like an economic recession that can have a real, but often temporary, impact on our opportunities. Instead, we're talking about the really big changes that irrevocably reshape the world we live in and how we sell.

The Macro Forces of Change

To understand this, we need to start with five important macro-level changes. You'll probably be familiar with each of these to some extent, but what we want to look at is how they are impacting the sales profession.

Digital first: disruption and consumption. The release of the latest smartphone technology certainly falls into this category, but it is much broader than that. McKinsey estimates that the Internet of Things has the potential to impact the global economy by as much as $11 trillion by 2025. This impact will be the result of changes in the way businesses collect and leverage data for better decision making and the way consumers use technology to interact with sellers. As sales becomes more technologically driven, desirable skill sets will shift from strictly soft skills like relationship building to include harder skills like data analysis. In some cases, the best candidates may not even come from the field of sales.

Emerging middle class. In the developed world, the number of people with middle-class buying power has remained relatively stagnant and, in some cases, has even declined. However, in many emerging economies the opposite is true. By 2025, the middle class is expected to have increased by 153% around the world, with the greatest increases coming from countries in the Asia-Pacific region. To tap into this new buying power, companies are going to have to staff a sales force with professionals from countries and cultures that may be very different from those of their current sales force. These new hires will have unique enablement needs.

Increased urbanization. Many geographies are also moving from primarily agrarian-based economies to heavily industrialized economies supported by growing cities. As many as 65 million people are moving to cities every year. That's the equivalent of adding seven new Chicagos (including surrounding suburbs), five-and-a-half new cities the size of the Paris metro area or almost two new cities to rival Shanghai every year! What were once small urban areas will grow into commerce power centers as people and industry flock to these cities in the hope of new opportunities and an improved lifestyle. Companies will need to adapt both their market and go-to-customer strategies to adapt to new opportunities and new competitors that are sure to emerge.

Productivity and the aging workforce. In more mature markets, workers are hitting retirement age faster than they can be replaced with new recruits. The labor market for the last 50 years has seen a steady growth of around 1.7%, but McKinsey predicts it will drop to just 0.3% over the next 50 years in its report *Global Growth: Can Productivity Save the Day in an Aging World?*

For businesses, this translates into more competition for an ever-smaller pool of qualified talent. To be successful, companies will need to get better at attracting younger talent and profiling new hires. Once talent is hired, enablement will need to onboard these new recruits as quickly as possible and provide the services necessary to drive sales professionals to higher and higher levels of productivity.

Invisible sector boundaries. The ability to redefine your industry has long been a recognizable principle of business survival. If you took any business classes at all, you probably remember the buggy whip manufacturer example or how railroad companies went out of business because they saw themselves as being in the railroad business and not the broader transportation market. Some of the most successful businesses today are masters at crossing sector boundaries. Ten years ago, Amazon just sold books. Today, the retail giant is successfully chipping away at established retail and logistics businesses across a range of sectors.

For sellers, the competitive landscape shifts like the sands of the Sahara. Salespeople will need to get better at crossing these boundaries, selling into new markets and competing against companies that they never imagined would enter their space.

Sales Is Changing at the Micro Level, Too

It's not just the macro forces that are impacting our ability to sell. There are a number of micro forces at work as well. If you're in sales, you probably have stories you could tell in each of these categories, but our research puts some statistics behind the changes you see every day.

More buyers involved. In complex B2B sales, facing a team of buyers is nothing new, but over the years, the size of that team has been steadily growing. Our 2018 research shows the number of buyers on the average buying team has risen to 6.4. Our clients also tell us that these teams are made up of buyers from a wider range of disciplines as well. Salespeople will need to get better at managing a larger number of buyers and identifying their unique challenges, wins and ideas for how to achieve their personal and business objectives.

Increasingly formalized process. As the size of the buying team increases, businesses tend to follow a more formalized process. This is one of the reasons we will focus so much on the path the customer follows to make decisions and implement solutions throughout the rest of this book.

Political and business-driven decisions. Increasing the number of people on the team almost always increases the amount of politics involved as interrelationship dynamics become more complex. Teams are also focused more on the business aspects of the decision, and the percentage of customers requiring an ROI analysis has gone from a five-year average of 40 to 61% in 2016.

Evolving buyer expectations and needs. Today's buyers have greater access to information than ever before, but while that may mean they are much *more* informed when they engage sales, it doesn't always mean they are *better* informed. Furthermore, buyers are not so much interested in what a product, service or solution *is* as what it *does.* They want to know how it will help them solve their challenges or reach a business goal. That requires a very different selling approach that translates capabilities into business value. This need cannot be met by adding a little bit of customer-centric color to an otherwise product-centric approach.

Longer sales cycles. The CSO Insights 2017 World-Class Sales Practices Study found that 60% of sales cycles with new customers lasted over six months. That's up from 41% just a year ago. This is reflective of other trends, such as larger buying teams, as well as the increasing sophistication of the solutions sold. While sales enablement can sometimes help shorten sales cycles, in general, salespeople and organizations will need to learn to adapt to their approach to these longer selling cycles.

The Rise of Sales Enablement

The changing needs of today's buyers and the downward slide in sales performance have led to an increased focus on sales

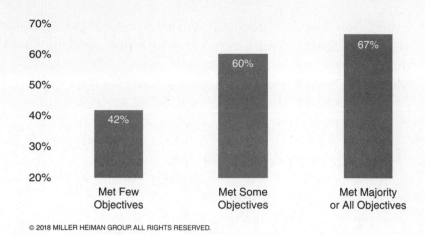

Figure I.1 Quota Attainment As Related to Sales Enablement Program Success

enablement in many organizations. In 2013, only 19% of companies we studied had a dedicated enablement person, program or function. In 2017, that rose to 59%.

How successful sales enablement is makes a huge difference. In our most recent study, only 35% of organizations reported that their enablement discipline met or exceeded expectations, but within this group, 67% of salespeople achieved quota (see Figure I.1). Organizations that reported meeting only some of their enablement expectations saw 60% of salespeople achieving quota. Organizations that reported achieving few of their expectations, essentially failing to enable their sales force, saw only 42% of their salespeople achieving quota. Quota attainment in this final group was even lower than the study's average quota attainment of 58%.

So, what's gone wrong?

CSO Insights research and our experiences in the field with hundreds of sales organizations lead us to several main conclusions:

- There is very little agreement (even within organizations) on what exactly sales enablement is, what it does and how to create an effective discipline.

- Even when there is agreement within the organization, most sales enablement initiatives are shaped around vague and unclear outcomes.
- Most sales enablement initiatives are not designed to help salespeople adapt to the micro and macro forces in the marketplace.

The goal of this book is to equip sales enablement professionals to create a sustainable, consistent enablement discipline that has a real impact on performance by developing the skills, knowledge and behaviors the sales force needs to succeed.

To that end, we've divided this book into five parts.

Part One: We'll lay the foundation by defining what enablement is and how it helps to improve performance.

Part Two: We'll introduce the Enablement Clarity Model, a framework that can help guide your efforts to create a scalable, adaptive discipline.

Part Three: We'll go deeper into the scope of services that enablement offers and how they must be aligned to be effective.

Part Four: We'll focus on how to create and deliver these services using a formalized, collaborative process. We'll also examine the role of technology and how to measure results.

Part Five: We'll give you a look at where the profession of sales is headed and how a formal sales force enablement discipline will be a must-have for future sales success.

This book is written for everyone from the sales enablement manager responsible for executing strategy to the executive looking for ways to improve performance. It is a collaborative effort of two authors:

Byron Matthews, Chief Executive Officer of Miller Heiman Group. Byron not only brings the senior leader's perspective to the topic of selling, he also has a long and successful track record in sales himself with major companies, including Aflac, Mercer and Accenture. In the industry, he is a sought-after speaker on topics such as AI-augmented sales and the future of selling.

Tamara Schenk, Research Director, CSO Insights. In addition to being the lead analyst for sales force enablement at CSO Insights, Tamara is a noted author, speaker and evangelist on the topic. She also brings real-world enablement experience to the table, having come up through the enablement ranks to serve as VP of Sales Enablement for T-Systems, a leading global IT and telecom company, before joining Miller Heiman Group.

We encourage you not just to read this book but to consider it a blueprint for action. Each chapter contains prescriptive advice, evidence to support our recommendations and actions you can take immediately as you start your journey toward sales enablement success. At the end of each chapter, we've also included questions to consider as you engage other stakeholders in your organization.

We've also set up an online resource center at www.miller heimangroup.com/salesenablementguidebook where you can get copies of our referenced reports as well as additional tools and resources. In addition to resources we mention in the book, we will also add additional materials as new research becomes available.

We wish you all the best!

Byron Matthews
Chief Executive Officer
Miller Heiman Group

Tamara Schenk
Research Director
CSO Insights

1

The Science of Selling

Key Points

- The science of selling helps sales enablement profession-als and business leaders understand what works, providing a clearer vision of how to enable performance.
- Relationship levels and sales processes contribute equally to sales success. Research shows that the higher the rela-tionship level and the more formal the process, the better the sales results.
- Sales enablement owns relationship practices and rein-forces defined processes.
- Perspective Selling is the next evolution of sales. Provid-ing perspectives helps buyers move forward and helps the seller move up the relationship axis in the SRP Matrix.

Is Selling Art or Science?

Thirty years ago, if you were to ask someone whether selling was an art or a science, they might have given you an odd look. The prevailing opinion was that selling was an art. Everybody knew selling was about relationships, and great salespeople were always "people people." Exactly how they did what they did was a bit of a mystery, but so long as they made their numbers, sales leadership didn't give it much thought.

Fast-forward a few decades, and sales leaders recognize that selling is just as much science as art. We now have the tools we need to track activities and behaviors and link them to results. We no longer need to guess at what works. We know what works, and we can prove it.

For enablement professionals, this is good news. Knowing what works means you can target your efforts more effectively. In this chapter, we'll dig into the science of selling to paint a clearer vision of what you are trying to enable.

The Relationship/Process Dynamic

Through our work with thousands of selling organizations, we've identified two critical levels of sales success: relationships and process. Each of these levels can be seen as a spectrum that describes the evolution of the organization.

Relationship Levels

Level 1 Approved Vendor. The organization is seen by the majority of its customers as a legitimate provider of the products or services it offers, but it is not recognized for having any significant, sustainable competitive edge over alternative offerings. Often the salesperson may sell the product using messages provided by marketing or product management, without thoroughly understanding what the customer is looking to accomplish. As information on products is easily accessible to customers, these are the kinds of relationships that rely less and less on sellers and are more likely to be replaced by artificial intelligence in the future.

Level 2 Preferred Supplier. Preferred suppliers add additional value by applying their knowledge of how clients use their products and services. In addition to standard features and benefits, they emphasize attributes like reliability and a proven track record. It's a step up from approved vendor status, but sellers at this level are still vulnerable to unseen competitive and market forces because the interaction between the buyer and seller remains largely transactional and product oriented.

Level 3 Solutions Consultant. Solutions consultants possess expertise that moves beyond their own organizations and products to a deeper understanding of their customers' businesses. Solutions consultants connect with their customers by asking questions about the challenges the customers are facing or the goals they want to achieve. Then, they connect their solutions to these needs. They help the customer envision how products work within the customer's business.

Level 4 Strategic Contributor. Strategic contributors have an even deeper knowledge of the customer: their industry, who they compete with, who their customers are and so on. This allows them to add additional value by providing perspectives the customer may not have. Strategic contributors are often invited to help the customer define the challenge or opportunity and possible options, giving them a definite advantage over the competition.

Level 5 Trusted Partner. Trusted partners are viewed as key to the customer's long-term success. Their knowledge of the customer is so deep and so wide that the value they offer isn't always limited to the immediate sale. Trusted partners are viewed by the customer as part of the customer's organization.

Strategic contributors and trusted partners have a clear edge on the competition. They are also in a better position to adapt their sales strategies to changes in the customer's business and the marketplace. But, while sales organizations may make

Levels 4 and 5 their goal, very few achieve it. Roughly 75% of organizations we've studied are at Level 3 or below.

Process Levels

Level 1 Random. This company lacks a single standard process for how it engages with prospects and customers. Salespeople are allowed to do their own thing their own way. So long as targets are met, no one asks too many questions. When a salesperson underperforms, management usually looks to replace the individual, not the processes. Companies at this level are always at a higher risk of missing targets because they are reliant on a few high performers who have figured it out.

Level 2 Informal. This company has a documented sales process, but if they're being honest, sales management will admit that not everyone follows it. Successful people are still allowed to do their own thing. Less successful salespeople are encouraged to follow the process, but since it's often based on old, product-oriented selling methodologies, this doesn't always lead to improved performance.

Level 3 Formal. This company has a defined sales process, and it is enforced—sometimes fanatically. Sales operations periodically conducts process reviews, using performance metrics and analyses (often generated from data in the CRM system) to determine where improvements are needed in adherence to the process or in the process itself.

While a formal process is far better than an informal or random approach, it can also have a certain rigidity that doesn't allow the salesperson to adapt to the situation or the changing macro and micro forces. In addition, formal processes tend to live only as long as the current methodology remains popular. Jumping from sales methodology to sales methodology based on the latest best-selling business book can be confusing to the sales team and lead to a lack of faith in sales methodologies in general.

Level 4 Dynamic. A dynamic process is formal, but it is characterized by its adaptability. Companies at this level focus on developing situational fluency in their salespeople, and their processes support it. Instead of reviewing the process once a year or with the release of the next bestseller, they use a constant stream of key performance indicators to provide an ongoing analysis and to detect the need to adapt the process to market changes long before others in their space. We'll talk about this more in Chapter 10 when we discuss enablement technology, but companies at this level will be among the first to leverage artificial intelligence in their processes.

In our latest studies, there was an even split between companies that had a random or informal process and those that had a formal or dynamic process. When we dig into this in one-on-one conversations with executives, most admit that no matter how much thought they put into defining a process they don't execute it as well as they would like.

The Sales Relationship Process (SRP) Matrix

Hopefully, after reading the previous discussion, you've been thinking about where your company falls on these two spectrums. If you're like most, you'd probably like to be considered a strategic contributor or trusted partner more often, and you know you need to formalize your processes a bit more. But is the effort worth it?

To answer this question, we combined relationship and process level with a Sales Relationship Process (SRP) Matrix and mapped thousands of sales organizations onto it to gauge the impact of relationship and process on performance. Let's first look at where companies fell on the matrix. It's probably no surprise that the bulk of organizations are in a zone we call Level 2. Their processes are somewhere between formal and informal, but rarely dynamic. Their relationships have progressed beyond the approved vendor stage, but few have made it to strategic

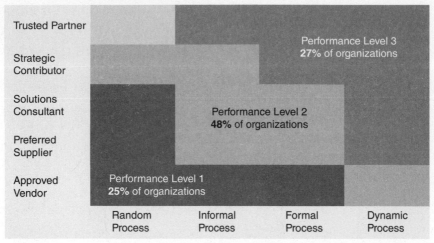

Figure 1.1 SRP Matrix Performance Levels

contributor and fewer still to trusted partner status. The rest of the organizations were split between Level 3 and Level 1 (see Figure 1.1).

To gauge performance for each of these levels, we used standard performance metrics that are meaningful to almost every organization: win rate, percent of salespeople achieving quota and percent of revenue attained. For each metric, we saw a striking difference in performance as we moved up levels (see Figure 1.2).

In most organizations, sales operations is responsible for defining, managing and measuring sales processes. Nevertheless, as we'll discuss throughout this book, sales enablement plays an

	Performance Level 1	Performance Level 2	Performance Level 3
% of Forecast Deals Won	41%	47%	53%
% of Salespeople Achieving Quota	47%	54%	60%
% Revenue Plan Attainment	84%	84%	89%

Figure 1.2 Results by SRP Matrix Performance Level

important role in facilitating and reinforcing those processes through the services it provides.

When it comes to relationships, sales enablement takes the lead. Its objective is to enable customer-facing professionals to add value in every interaction. Adding value is how organizations drive to ever-higher levels of performance. While it doesn't own responsibility for the sales process, sales enablement must design its services with the defined sales process in mind. In turn, this helps reinforce the process.

Leveling Up on the SRP Matrix

After establishing where you are on the SRP Matrix, it's a natural next step to consider what you need to do to move up a level. In our *2017 World Class Sales Practices Study*, we examined over 60 sales practices to understand which were most strongly linked to sales results and then boiled them down to the top 12, as shown in Table 1.1.

As you can see from the list, these include a range of practices that require investments in skills, processes, systems and technologies. Many of these practices, such as "our salespeople consistently and effectively articulate a solution that is aligned to the customer's needs," are practices that are directly impacted by the strength of the organization's enablement efforts.

With this list established, we then combed through the 1,300 organizations that participated in the study to look for those World-Class organizations that strongly excelled in at least 10 of the 12. As you might expect, at only 7% of organizations in our study, this is an exclusive club indeed.

These organizations consistently outperformed the entire population of respondents. For example, the percentage of salespeople achieving quota averaged out to 53% when looking at all responses. When we segmented out just those who met the definition of World-Class, the percentage rose to 70%, right at the 65% to 70% level recommended by most sales experts. (Too many

Table 1.1 Top 12 World-Class Practices

1   Our salespeople consistently and effectively articulate a solution that is aligned to the customer's needs.

2   We deliver a consistent customer experience that lives up to and aligns with our brand promise.

3   We continually assess why our top performers are successful.

4   When we lose a salesperson (voluntary/involuntary) we consistently determine the reasons why.

5   We effectively collect and share best practices across our sales and service organizations.

6   Our sales managers are held accountable for the effective use of sales tools and resources by the sales force.

7   Our salespeople consistently and effectively communicate appropriate value messages, aligned to the customer's needs.

8   Our culture supports continuous development of salespeople and sales leaders.

9   Our organization consistently develops and ensures implementation of personalized performance improvement plans.

10   Customers have consistently positive interactions with us regardless of which channel(s) they use to work with us.

11   Our sales teams are effective at surfacing the specific reasons why certain customers stop doing business with us.

12   We are effective at selling value to avoid discounting or gaining comparative value in return for price concessions.

---

salespeople at quota is a strong indication that quotas were not set high enough.)

In our final stage of analysis, we plotted the 7% of World-Class performers onto the SRP Matrix. As you would expect, the majority are in Level 3. However, the analysis revealed that not all World-Class performers achieved the highest levels of relationship and process success. In Figure 1.3, each dot represents one of the World-Class participants.

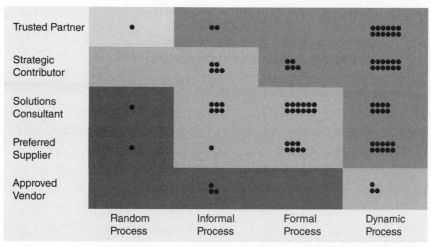

Figure 1.3 Distribution of World-Class Organizations Across SRP Matrix Levels

World-Class Isn't the Same for Everyone

While moving up levels on the SRP Matrix can impact performance, not every organization can or should aim for Level 3. Here are a couple of examples.

> A *small law firm.* In a law firm or other small consultancy, those who manage client service and delivery are often responsible for selling these services as well. Long-term relationships with clients are key, and while the sales process is often informal or random, the relationship level would be considered one of trusted adviser due to the nature of the service.

World-Class for this type of organization is going to be high on the relationship axis, but not so far to the right on the process axis. When the organization is small, with limited growth goals, this works. The problem is that it doesn't scale if the consultancy decides it wants to expand, and it will have to invest in maturing its processes to maintain its World-Class status.

A *large organization selling commodities*. On the other end of
the spectrum is the large organization selling commodity
products. A good example might be a paper products manufacturer. These products are important, but they aren't
necessarily of strategic value. Cost and availability often
drive the decision to buy, and the buying cycle may consist of nothing more than the procurement team reaching out to various vendors for information on pricing and
lead times.

For an organization like this, preferred supplier status may
be as high as it will ever get on the relationship axis. However,
through constant analysis of the market and needs of customers,
the sales organization can identify and codify the processes that
work and drive to World-Class levels of success. In the event this
organization acquires another organization with more strategic
services, it is better prepared to fully leverage the opportunity
because of the formality of its processes.

The Evolution of Sales

So far in this chapter, we've introduced the SRP Matrix and
how moving up levels is linked to better performance. Then,
we talked about the behaviors World-Class organizations consistently exhibit. Before we dive into enablement, we need to talk
about how sales has evolved and how clinging to outdated sales
methodologies can keep you from moving to ever-higher levels of
performance.

There have been hundreds of sales methodologies introduced
over the years, but most of those in the modern era (post-
industrial age) can be grouped into one of three stages:

1. *Product.* Before the internet was at everybody's fingertips,
   buyers came to a salesperson needing product information, including detailed specs, because they couldn't get
   it anywhere else. Aside from the random word-of-mouth

recommendation, many buyers had no idea what their options even were. They came to a salesperson expecting to be educated on products, including sitting through sometimes daylong demonstrations. The salesperson's role was that of product expert. They had to quickly understand the customer's issues and then match the product to the need.

2. *Features/benefits.* Slowly, sellers discovered that the best sales-people were those who could translate the features of the product into the benefits the customers were looking for. No doubt, this had been the case for decades, but the features/benefits stage formalized the approach. A ton of work was done creating "pain chains" and "feature/benefit state-ments," but at the end of the day, selling still revolved around the product.

3. *Solution/consultative selling.* The first real leap away from product-focused selling came with the concept of Solution Selling. In Solution Selling, the salesperson uses diagnostic skills to understand the customer's objectives. Instead of just telling customers about the features and benefits of their prod-ucts and letting the customer sort it all out, consultative sales-people match solutions to the customer's needs and put their proposals in the language of the buyers.

As you read through these descriptions, you probably noticed a correlation to the relationship spectrum we discussed earlier. Organizations that are still at the approved vendor level often follow an outdated product-oriented approach to selling. Moving to features/benefits selling can help you break to the next level, but you won't get much beyond preferred supplier. Solution/consultative selling is squarely in line with Level 3, the solutions consultant.

But one of the reasons few companies manage to break through to become strategic contributors or trusted partners is that they haven't evolved to the next stage: Perspective Selling.

Perspective Selling: The Next Step in the Evolution of Sales

In a hyper-informed world, sales professionals need to approach buyers differently. Buyers come to the table armed with information (and misinformation) as well as preconceived notions about what your product does and does not do and how you compare to the competition. This makes for a challenging sales environment if buyers' understanding of their challenges and their concepts of a potential solution aren't aligned to what you have to offer.

> The successful sales professional adds perspective by combining deep knowledge of the customer, their challenges and their desired results with the experience and insights gained from working with similar customers and their knowledge of potential solutions.

The successful sales professional adds perspective by combining deep knowledge of the customer, their challenges and their desired results with the experience and insights gained from working with similar customers and their knowledge of potential solutions. They also bring in expertise in the form of research, thought leadership and subject matter experts to help buyers see their challenges and opportunities in new ways. We call this Perspective Selling, and it can be applied at every phase of the customer's path.

We'll get deeper into the customer's path in Chapter 3, but for now, think of it as the process the customer follows to approach a challenge or opportunity, gather information, make a decision and implement the solution.

While the customer is still gathering information, sales professionals can ask strategic questions and provide thought-provoking insights and information to guide the customer's thinking and help them explore areas they hadn't thought about. Adding perspective helps prospects and customers understand the real business impact of their challenges and what outcomes they could achieve if they decide to change their current state. If they don't commit to change—and they are only likely to do so when the perspective the salesperson offers shows measurable business value in metrics that matter to them—they will never progress to the buying phase.

As customers move toward buying, the sales professional can provide further evidence that helps them assess how best to solve their challenge or reach their goal. Perspective Selling is even applicable after the sale is closed, as the sales professional can offer perspective to help the customer recognize the value that has been delivered.

Solution Selling Didn't Die; It Evolved

In June of 2012, *Harvard Business Review* published an article in which the authors declared "The End of Solution Sales." The piece anointed "insight selling" as the successor, executed by sellers who profile as "challengers." This method, notable for "creating tension" as a selling trait and working to "upend your customers' ways of thinking" was described as being in direct opposition to Solution Sales.

In reality, Solution Selling is not dead. Its tenets, such as helping customers surface needs they weren't originally aware of and using questioning skills to help customers process through their opportunities and problems, are still very effective methods. These methods have been combined with techniques for providing perspective to customers to expand the nature of interactions, and ultimately, relationships. This has evolved Solution Selling into a more value-added, business-level approach called Perspective Selling.

Why evolve Solution Selling into Perspective Selling rather than abandon it in favor of something completely different?

- Perspective Selling works with a range of seller types. There are too many variables to define one universal successful seller profile. Success profiles vary by industry, selling environment, sales type, customer segments and more. They should be built in the context of a specific sales organization, not broadly defined.

- It works with a range of customer types. According to Miller Heiman Group research, there are five unique decision-making styles. Each prefers information to be presented differently depending on how they consume data and how they use that data to make decisions. With more than five sellers and five buyers involved in a typical complex sale, agility and adaptability are required to manage sharing insights with a mix of styles.

- It provides multiple ways to capture a customer's interest. There are many ways to provide insights to a customer, and not all are contrarian. Miller Heiman Group methodologies have long emphasized value drivers such as helping customers become aware of unrecognized needs or opportunities, expanding the customer's definition of success and educating the customer on new solutions.

- It uses conversation and relationships as the broader context. Disruptive information can certainly deepen relationships, but only after establishing credibility first. Sellers must earn the right to share potentially provocative information with their customers if they want that information to help guide thinking versus destroy rapport.

- It works in a range of selling scenarios. Selling is not just for new customers. In fact, CSO Insights research shows that an average of 68% of revenues come from existing customers. Customers in the implementation phase of a buy cycle or those considering renewing their purchase derive more value from aligned support than disruptive content.

Sales organizations are best served by defining a successful talent profile, selecting an adaptable sales methodology, defining a dynamic sales process and building out an enablement road map. Sales enablement is in the unique position to help drive and align these activities to ensure that they are tightly integrated to selling realities.

A Framework for Performance

Now that we know how to impact performance, we better understand what we need to enable.

But what exactly is sales enablement? And how do we do it? Many organizations set themselves up for failure by launching sales enablement initiatives without giving much thought to what sales enablement is and how to be successful. Sure, they think about the results they are trying to achieve, but not a lot about what kind of approach will get them to their desired outcomes.

In Part Two, we'll start by defining sales force enablement so we have a common understanding of what it is. Then, we'll provide the framework that will serve as the structure for the rest of this book and your enablement discipline.

Questions to Consider

- Where does our organization fit today on the SRP Matrix? What evidence do we have to support our conclusions?
- What would our ideal position be and why?
- Which of the 12 World-Class practices do we consistently demonstrate?
- How are we using sales enablement to improve customer relationships and reinforce processes?
- How well do we equip our sales professionals to add valuable, relevant perspectives in every interaction with prospects and customers?

PART

II

Laying the Foundation

As we mentioned in our introduction, many of the organizations we work with don't have a common definition of what sales enablement is. Sure, each individual contributor has their own concept, but sometimes those concepts are so far apart that any discussion is fruitless.

To avoid falling into that trap, we'll start Part Two by providing a common definition that describes what sales enablement is and why we call it sales force enablement, its purpose, how it reaches its goals and for whom these services are offered. It is based on research, our experiences helping clients and our experiences having been sales enablement professionals ourselves and will serve as a common foundation for our discussion—and any discussions you have within your organization.

But definitions aren't enough. Just knowing what something is and what it's for doesn't tell us how to create it. Having a model as a practical guide will help you build your discipline step by step, so first, we'll take a bird's-eye view of the many facets of enablement by introducing the Sales Force Enablement Clarity

Model. Then, in Chapters 3 and 4, we'll start laying the foundation for your enablement discipline by taking an up-close look at the foundational facets of the clarity model. Getting these facets right will set you off on a path toward success.

As we stated in Part One, this book is designed to help you implement the concepts you've learned. In each chapter, we'll continue to include questions to consider as well as additional models, actions and advice that will help get your sales force enablement efforts off the ground.

2

The Many Facets of Sales
Force Enablement

Key Points

- A common definition of sales enablement is a prerequisite to having a productive discussion on how to enable sales.
- While many teams contribute to enablement efforts, enablement professionals can ensure consistency and effectiveness by orchestrating the efforts of multiple collaborators.
- To be effective, enablement must be seen as a strategic discipline that is set apart from other functions such as marketing and training, even though those functions contribute to enablement.
- The Sales Force Enablement Clarity Model provides a framework for assembling a holistic, effective sales force enablement discipline, and every facet of the model correlates to an improvement in performance.

What Is Sales Force Enablement?

After an important meeting, has anyone ever joked that "we're still confused, but on a higher level"? We've all experienced those situations where we're talking at cross-purposes with those we want to engage, educate or persuade.

> "Before I came here, I was confused about this subject. Having listened to your lecture, I am still confused—but on a higher level."
>
> *Enrico Fermi*
> Physicist and inventor of the
> world's first nuclear reactor

In business, it's often not our philosophical or intellectual differences that separate us so much as our understanding of the core terms and phrases we all use. In discussions with clients about their sales enablement discipline, we've often had to stop the conversation and confirm that everyone has the same understanding of what we mean.

Having a common definition to anchor our discussions is a tremendous help. Here's one we developed that has served our clients well:

*Sales Force Enablement: A strategic, collaborative discipline
designed to increase predictable sales results
by providing consistent, scalable enablement services
that allow customer-facing professionals and their managers
to add value in every customer interaction.*

We don't need to dissect the definition line by line, but there are a few points we want to call attention to here.

Sales force enablement is a strategic discipline. It is not a one-off initiative or something that is assigned to a team as an ancillary task. Organizations live and die based on the success of their sales force. It only makes sense that enabling them be considered one of the highest priorities.

Sales force enablement doesn't end with sales professionals. While the field sales role is often the primary focus of enablement, selling involves many more people in the organization. Sales *force* enablement is about enabling *anyone* in the organization who engages the customer. This certainly includes sales and service staff. It also includes functions like marketing that interact with customers, sometimes directly and sometimes through sales. For some organizations, the focus could even include enabling the team members who staff the reception desk to better serve the customers who visit your facilities.

Enabling roles beyond sales is a hallmark of a World-Class sales organization, but given where most organizations are today, our focus in this book is going to be on enabling sales roles.

Sales managers must be included. Sales managers are responsible for ensuring go-to-customer strategies are carried out effectively, so they need to be enabled, too. Sales enablement can provide a sales tool to a sales professional, but if this individual's manager is not also versed on how the tool should be used in the field and cannot coach to drive reinforcement and adoption, you put your initial enablement investments at risk.

You don't need to do everything. If you're a sales enablement professional, this point should be welcome news. Most sales enablement organizations don't have the staff or resources to do everything. Enablement will require the efforts of individuals and teams across the organization. In later chapters, we'll talk a great deal about how to set up a collaborative discipline.

Navigating Complexity

Living up to this definition can seem like a monumental under-taking, especially for those sales force enablement leaders who haven't yet gained the necessary organizational support. It's important to remember that this definition describes an ideal enablement discipline and that reaching this ideal will take time. Your starting point as well as your goals and how you reach them will be different from every other organization. And that's okay, too!

While people will counsel you to "keep it simple," keep in mind that they aren't necessarily talking about your discipline. What they want are enablement services that are easy to use, but that doesn't mean that they are effortless to create. Your journey will be a challenging one—cross-functional collaboration is sel-dom easy—but as you'll see in the real-world examples and the research we provide, the effort is worth it.

The Sales Force Enablement Clarity Model

Think about your last big project, sales enablement or otherwise. You probably spent a lot of time in meetings with other stakehold-ers, trying to gain clarity on the goals of the project, the overall approach, the status and the next steps. Without clarity, every-one does their own thing, and the project outcome falls far short of expectations.

The Sales Force Enablement Clarity Model (see Figure 2.1) brings a common focus to the sales force enablement discipline. In this chapter, we're going to provide a quick description of each of the facets. Then, in subsequent chapters, we'll discuss individ-ual facets in more detail, providing guidance on how to approach that facet in your organization.

We use a diamond to represent our model for several reasons, the main one being that you will never find a smooth, polished diamond in nature. All diamonds come out of the ground looking nothing like the finished product we see displayed in the jeweler's case. Likewise, your sales force enablement discipline will also

Figure 2.1 The Sales Force Enablement Clarity Model

require lots of effort to get it into the smooth, polished shape you need it to be.

Furthermore, only about 2% of the diamonds mined are considered flawless. The percentage of flawless sales enablement disciplines is even lower—there are none. Nevertheless, the value of a diamond is easily recognizable even in a flawed state. The same can be said of sales force enablement. Don't let your pursuit of (unattainable) perfection keep you from moving forward.

Finally, most diamonds have lots of facets and that makes them the perfect choice for representing the many facets of an effective sales enablement discipline. Let's examine each of these under our loupe.

Customer. Customers don't immediately notice how perfectly you execute your sales methodology, how flawless your content is or how well-trained your salespeople are. The first thing they will notice (and sometimes the only thing) is how well your sales team understands them: their role, their challenges, their industry and what they want to achieve. For that reason, the customer is at the top of our clarity model and must be reflected in every enablement service you provide. In the age of the customer, your sales force can only be successful by working with customers based on their context and the way they view their challenges and potential solutions.

Seeing things from the customer's point of view requires outside-in thinking. When you're designing enablement services, put yourself in their shoes. If the service, such as a piece of content, is designed to be used with a customer, what would you think of it? Remember to look at the entire customer's path. In your mind's eye, see yourself traveling their path. Are you seeing relevance and value from your interactions at each step of the way?

Customer's path: The process the customer follows to approach a challenge or opportunity, gather information, make a decision and implement the solution. The path is unique for each buying decision the customer makes and not always linear.

Customer-facing professionals and their managers. While customers are at the top of our clarity model as enablement's main design point, enablement services must also be aligned to the needs of the organization. This includes all individuals who have customer-facing roles as well as their managers. This is the main reason we call it sales *force* enablement in our definition, although this is one of those aspects of the definition that is more easily accomplished in a mature sales enablement practice. To be very clear: Customer-facing professionals and their managers are enablement's target audience. They are enablement's customers.

Sponsorship, strategy and charter. Next, we'll drop down to the bottom of our diamond and look at its foundation. Of course, you need to start with a strategy, but even the best sales force enablement initiatives fail if the team has the responsibility but not the authority to enact the strategy. This includes gaining the all-important executive sponsorship.

Sales Force Enablement's Impact on Performance

The Sales Force Enablement Clarity Model was born out of more than a decade of research conducted by CSO Insights. In the following table, we've highlighted some of the correlations between the facets and performance improvements, which we'll be discussing in greater detail throughout the book.

Facet	Impact on Performance*
Customer	Dynamic alignment to the customer's path correlated to a 10% improvement in win rates and a 14% improvement in quota attainment.
Customer-facing professionals and their managers	A formal coaching process improved win rates for forecast deals by 14% compared to the 2017 study's average win rate of 52%. A dynamic coaching process correlated to a 28% improvement in win rates as compared to the average.
Sponsorship, strategy and charter	Organizations with a formal charter-based approach to enablement achieved 74% of quota compared to the study's average of 58%. Organizations with an ad hoc or project-based approach achieved only 43% of quota.

(*continued*)

Facet	Impact on Performance*
Effective enablement services	Effective content services correlated to an 8% improvement in quota attainment, while effective training services improved quota attainment between 18% and 22%. Effective coaching services had the greatest impact with up to 28% better win rates for forecast deals.
Formalized collaboration	A formal cross-functional collaboration approach correlated to a 7% improvement in quota attainment.
Integrated enablement technology	Organizations that share content via e-mail or multiple repositories achieve an average quota attainment of 57%, whereas organizations that share content with enablement technology and/or integrated into their CRM achieve 63%.
Efficient enablement operations	Our studies have not yet looked directly at the impact of enablement operations on performance, but as you'll see in Part Four, effective enablement operations are an imperative for achieving the performance improvements correlated to the other facets of the clarity model.

*All results are from Miller Heiman Group and CSO Insights 2017 studies.

In the middle of our diamond are four facets that cover enablement services, collaboration, technology and operations. While the top and bottom facets cover strategy and approach, these facets address the inner mechanics of the sales force enablement discipline.

Effective enablement services. These are the services the discipline provides to allow the organization to reach its desired results. If you think about your internal customers, this is the only facet they see. If someone outside the organization were to ask a customer-facing professional what sales enablement does, it's likely that they would talk about these services. We'll discuss enablement services in detail in Chapters 5, 6 and 7.

The remaining three inner facets focus on the mechanics necessary to design, produce and deliver these services as well as manage the discipline. When we talk about moving from a random discipline to one that is dynamic, we are often focusing on these facets. They are essential to the stability and scalability of your efforts.

Formalized collaboration. Enablement professionals must *orchestrate* the process of creating and delivering enablement services by enlisting the aid of many other functions within the organization. As simple as this sounds, it's one of the critical takeaways from this book. Your sales force enablement initiative will fail if you try to do it all. We'll spend a lot of time talking about the importance of collaboration and how to go about orchestrating the development and delivery of enablement services.

Integrated enablement technology. Sales enablement technology is *not* the same thing as sales enablement, but these days, the right enablement technologies, deployed in the right ways, can extend your competitive advantage. We'll even go so far as to say that if you don't have a strong technology strategy supporting your sales force enablement efforts, you're putting your organization at a distinct disadvantage.

Efficient enablement operations. We'll end our discussion on the individual facets of sales force enablement with a look at the management of sales force enablement and how to build sales force enablement into a strategic discipline in your organization. Enablement operations is often seen as a "black box" because it includes the behind-the-scenes functions of the discipline, but this is where all the enablement magic happens. As it is poorly understood, it is also a facet that is often overlooked. To ensure you don't fall into that trap, we'll discuss an enablement governance model and an enablement production process. We will also answer important questions such as: *How do we know if it's working?*

Who Owns Enablement?

Sales enablement is a fast-growing discipline: In 2013, 19% of participants in the CSO *Insights Sales Performance Optimization Study* reported having an enablement initiative or function. In 2016, that percentage had grown to 33%. In 2017, the number was 59%. Before we can go deeper into the facets of sales force enablement, we probably ought to address the question that's undoubtedly on everyone's mind: Who owns enablement?

We're starting to see more and more sales enablement functions report directly into senior leadership. In our 2016 research, 61% of sales enablement teams reported into senior sales management. In 2017, that percentage rose to 73%. We're even seeing an increasing number of functions report into the CRO and CEO functions, indicating that sales enablement is starting to receive recognition as a strategic discipline in many organizations. That's a good sign!

Enablement is still seen as a sales operations function in 18% of organizations, though these percentages are on a definite downward slide. Another good sign. In our work, we see this most commonly in large organizations that have an established, strategic sales operations function.

Although the percentage of enablement disciplines housed in other functions, such as sales training, learning and development and marketing, are on a downward slide as well, the percentages still registered in our research (see Figure 2.2). We find this placement more common in organizations where sales enablement is initiated and focused on one domain only such as content or training.

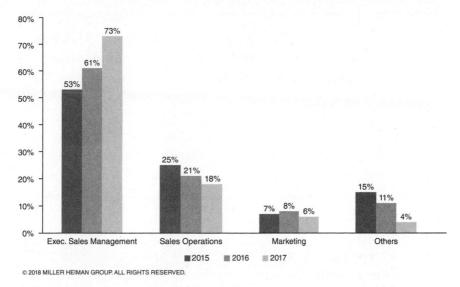

Figure 2.2 Sales Enablement: Reporting Structure 2015–2017

Examining the Facets

Next up, we're going to take a look at each of the facets of the Sales Force Enablement Clarity Model, beginning with the one that reflects the reason we are in business in the first place: the customer. Everything enablement does needs to be designed with the customer in mind, so it's essential to get this one right.

Questions to Consider

- How do we define enablement in our organization?
- How has our current reporting structure helped or hindered the development of sales enablement as a strategic discipline?
- If we were to diagram our current sales force enablement framework, what would it look like?
- For each facet of the Sales Force Enablement Clarity Model, which teams are responsible, and how do we ensure their efforts are integrated into the whole?

- Which facets of the Sales Force Enablement Clarity Model have we overlooked or not given enough focus? How has that hindered our effectiveness?

Immediate Actions

Jot down two or three immediate actions you can take to better define enablement in your organization and provide clarity for the discipline.

3

The Customer's Path

Key Points

- The customer's path is the process the customer follows to approach a challenge or opportunity, gather information, make a decision and implement a solution.
- Each buying team follows a unique path for each buying decision, and that path can change as the opportunity moves through the funnel.
- Since customers are the sole arbiter for when an opportunity moves forward, the customer's path serves as the primary design point for enablement.
- Enablement must provide services for each phase of the customer's path.
- Dynamic alignment to the customer's path can improve win rates by as much as 10% and quota attainment by as much as 14%.

Customers Are the Primary "Design Point" for Enablement

When we listen to sales enablement discussions, it's sometimes astonishing how little focus is on the customer. There is a great deal of talk about the sales process and how the sales enablement team needs to support that process, but very little talk about the customer's path: the process the customer follows to approach a challenge or opportunity, gather information, make a decision and implement a solution.

The internet has had a fundamental impact on the customer's path and the role a sales professional plays. Because of the vast amount of information available to buyers, salespeople rarely enjoy the information advantage they once had. To differentiate themselves from competing salespeople and solutions, the sales professionals need to add value by helping buyers understand what a product, service or solution means in terms that are relevant to them. Buyers are still the arbiters of how and when they move forward through the sales funnel, and no amount of customer calls, demonstrations or proposals is going to move customers forward until *they* are ready. Sales force enablement's role is to provide enablement services that equip the sales professional to add the value the customer needs at each stage.

One of the aspects of selling that makes this particularly challenging is that no two customers' paths are identical. A small-restaurant owner looking to expand is going to follow a very different path than the one taken by the buying team of a Fortune 500 company looking for a new employee health insurance provider.

It gets even more complicated when you consider that the path the Fortune 500 company follows to contract with a new insurance provider will be very different from the path another buying team in the same organization takes to procure office furniture for the new space in Dublin. Furthermore, the buying team for the office space in Dublin will follow a different path than a similar team buying furniture for an office in Sydney.

There's a time element involved as well. Like the commuter who needs to take a different route to work to avoid an unforeseen traffic jam or new construction, the path an individual buying team takes is heavily influenced by that team's environment. This includes the macro and micro market forces we talked about in the introduction as well as the dynamics within the organization.

Helping sales professionals align to the ever-changing customer's path is one of the biggest challenges sales force enablement professionals have. Nevertheless, the impact is significant. The *CSO Insights 2017 World-Class Sales Practices Study* found that improving alignment could improve win rates by as much as 10% and quota attainment by as much as 14%. This is the reason we talk about customers (and the customer's path) as the "design point" for enablement services.

"A few years ago, we did a lot of research to get the design point of our enablement practice right. We wanted to figure out what was out there, what was needed, and we also wanted to discover our gaps. So, we interviewed all involved departments, and we interviewed customers. Then we realized that there wasn't much of a connection between what the customers really wanted and what we were producing. We learned that we had to ensure that we are looking at our customers first because, at the end of the day, our sales force has to be successful working with our prospects and customers. We want our customers to fully understand what we are offering and what kind of value we can provide mapped to their specific context."

Christine Dorrion, CallidusCloud,
VP Global Sales & Channel
Operations and Enablement

A Common Framework

Despite the uniqueness of each customer's path, at a higher level, there are three phases that are common to every customer:

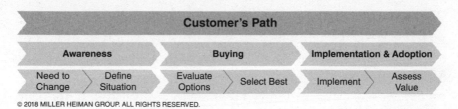

Figure 3.1 The Customer's Path

Awareness, Buying and Implementation and Adoption. As we move forward, we will use these three phases as a reference point for our discussions (see Figure 3.1).

In the awareness phase, buyers are still defining their challenges and opportunities, identifying possible ways of addressing them and gathering information about potential solutions. As many sellers are painfully aware, with the amount of information that can be gathered online, today's buyers are engaging sales later and, depending on the complexity of their challenge, differently in this phase.

Some organizations don't think much about the types of services sales needs in the awareness phase because they consider it the purview of the marketing team. Yet, the reality is that no matter how excellent marketing's lead generation efforts may be, sales needs to take responsibility for prospecting to ensure they have a full funnel. In some organizations, sales generates as much as 80% or more of their own business. Enablement is more important than ever in the awareness phase because it helps salespeople engage with prospects earlier and prepares them to be relevant, valuable and differentiating in every interaction.

> Enablement is more important than ever in the awareness phase because it helps salespeople engage with prospects earlier and prepares them to be relevant, valuable and differentiating in every interaction.

The buying phase is where salespeople want to invest their energy, and it is the phase most enablement teams focus on when providing content and training services. At this phase, sales is asked to demonstrate why their solution is the best, answer questions, create proposals, overcome obstacles, and above all, close the deal. Furthermore, they need to do all of this while establishing a long-term relationship with their customer.

The last stage, implementation and adoption, highlights one of the biggest differences between the Perspective Selling approach and some of the earlier buying/selling models. In fact, you might be surprised to see this phase included in a book on *sales* enablement. After all, isn't implementation of the solution the purview of the service team?

We include it for three reasons:

1. Sales professionals have to stay involved to ensure that the value that has been sold gets delivered, and they have to ensure that they communicate this back to their various involved buyers. This account-based approach creates the foundation for future business.
2. Sales professionals need to stay involved so that they can develop relationships within their accounts and identify new ways of adding value. Again, this is essential to future business opportunities.
3. Other customer-facing personnel, such as implementers and service professionals, can be very important when it comes to creating additional revenue and ensuring renewals. While they may not have a sales title, these professionals can be some of your best salespeople when properly equipped.

The customer's path is always changing, even after they have made a buying decision. Staying involved in the implementation and adoption phase helps salespeople remain aware of these changes and puts them in the best position to take advantage of new opportunities and to protect their accounts from being poached by the competition.

The CSO Insights Maturity Scale

As with the customer's path, no two organizations follow the same path toward World-Class performance. Yet we can benchmark the levels an organization typically goes through as it seeks to mature each facet of its enablement discipline. This helps leaders map the route they need to take and the milestones they need to reach along the way.

As we discuss the various facets of sales force enablement, this benchmarking will come up again and again. To help avoid confusion between the maturity levels for different facets of development, we use a common four-point scale: random, informal, formal and dynamic. Whenever we use this scale, we will explain the exact meaning in the same context as we did when we first introduced it to talk about sales process maturity in relation to the SRP Matrix in Chapter 1.

Why the Customer's Path Matters

Research shows just how much the customer's path and the alignment of your internal processes, including sales, services and marketing, to each phase of the customer's path matters. In the *2017 Sales Enablement Optimization Study*, CSO Insights broke customer path alignment down into four levels:

1. *Random*: The sales process is not aligned to the customer's path, and funnel review discussions almost always center around the internally defined sales process. Progress is seen in terms of sales activities: customer meetings, demonstrations, proposals and so on.
2. *Informal*: The customer's path is acknowledged, but there is no focused effort to align to it. The salesperson may discuss how the customer will make the decision and implement the solution at the beginning of the sale and refer back to it occasionally, but progress is still measured in terms of an internally

defined sales process and not in terms of the customer's path and *the customer's* decision to move forward.

3. *Formal*: The sales process has been mapped to the customer's path and internal processes and systems have been adjusted. During one-on-one opportunity reviews, the discussions focus more on where customers are on their paths and less on the sales cycle. However, the approach is rather ridged, with less flexibility in the unique path each buying team follows and the changes that occur.

4. *Dynamic*: The sales process is derived from the customer's path, changes along the customer's path can be detected early on (increasingly using technology), and selling processes evolve as the market or customer behaviors change.

The *2017 World-Class Sales Practices Study* found that the better the customer's path alignment, the better the sales results. Specifically, win rates improved by 10% and quota attainment by 14% versus the overall survey population when the organization dynamically aligned its sales processes to the customer's path.

Drilling deeper, the *2017 Sales Enablement Optimization Study* uncovered that only 21% of survey respondents had reached this level of alignment. In fact, over half (54%) of the study participants had either not aligned their selling processes to the customer's path or only aligned them informally. Sales force enablement leaders looking to gain a competitive advantage might want to mark customer's path alignment as an item for immediate action.

Methodology Connects the Sales Process to the Customer's Path

Your sales methodology can help you move from informal to formal alignment to the customer's path and then to dynamic, or it can hinder your progress. To better understand the connection between sales methodology and the customer's path, let's look at it in the context of process, methodology and skills. These terms are often used synonymously, or at least seen as overlapping, but there are important distinctions.

A *sales process* is a defined set of activities in a certain sequence to create and close deals, ideally mapped to the customer's path. This is where we might find the answers to questions like what is a qualified lead? And when does an opportunity hit the forecast? The sales process is usually defined by sales operations, with enablement's primary role being one of providing services that help reinforce adherence to the defined process.

Your *sales methodologies* tell you what to do at each step of the process, how to do it and why. For example, a sales process might define the steps that should be followed to prepare for a sales call. Methodology adds details such as how to perform an analysis of the network of impacted stakeholders in a particular selling situation, why this is important and how to apply the results of your analysis. Methodologies allow you to deeply understand your customer's path and to engage with buyers accordingly.

Your overall methodology might be made up of individual methodologies for different aspects of the sale. You might also have different methodologies for different markets or customer segments. For example, many of our methodologies such as Conceptual Selling® and Strategic Selling®, can be broadly applied, but our Large Account Management Process℠ is specifically designed for large and strategic accounts.

Lastly, *sales skills* are the capabilities that have to be developed so that a salesperson can follow the processes and apply the methodologies correctly and successfully. For example, to apply a methodology for uncovering latent business needs, a sales professional might need to develop their questioning skills, including understanding how to ask the right questions, how to listen to the answers (hearing what isn't said as well), and how to ask additional clarifying questions.

In summary, process defines the steps, methodology provides the what, why and how, and skills are what allow sales professionals to follow the steps and the methodologies successfully. That said, one of the most important points to take away from this discussion is that sales methodologies connect your sales processes to your customer's path.

> "Sales enablement is not end-customer facing. The sales directors, sales managers, all sales roles, these are the customers of sales enablement. However, the only people who can close the deals and deliver the quarterly numbers are the frontline salespeople with the appropriate governance of their sales management."
>
> *Robert Racine, Sales Enablement Leader*

Assessing the Needs of Your Sales Team

When we call the customer the design point for enablement, in no way are we saying that the needs of the sales organization are any less important. What we are saying is that the needs of your sales force should always be addressed within the context of your customer's path. As we go through each of the facets in the Sales Force Enablement Clarity Model, we will continue to keep customers as our design point while we focus more deeply on how to assess, prioritize and fulfill the needs of your sales force.

In the next chapter, we'll drop down to the bottom of the clarity model to look at another very important facet: the enablement charter. This charter not only serves as your business plan, but it is also the tool you will use to gain buy-in and support from senior leadership in your organization.

Questions to Consider

- How well do our enablement services help our salespeople be relevant, valuable and differentiating in every interaction with customers and prospects?

- How well are our enablement services aligned to the customer's path?
- Are we providing more services for one phase than others? If so, why is this? (For example, a siloed, functional approach or lack of collaboration between contributors.)

Immediate Actions

Jot down two or three immediate actions you can take to better align your enablement efforts to the customer's path.

4

The Enablement Charter

Key Points

- A charter (and the process of its creation) leads to clarity regarding enablement goals, strategies, services and results, and ensures executive sponsorship and buy-in.
- Having a charter can substantially impact sales enablement success—both real and perceived.
- Once approved, your charter continues to live on as your guide and can help keep you on track to achieving your vision.

What a Difference a Charter Makes!

Your charter functions as your business plan and is your guide for turning a random sales enablement effort into a formal, scalable and strategic sales force enablement discipline that has a definable, positive impact on the business. It is also the tool you use to sell enablement internally—the discipline itself or specific initiatives—to senior executives. As you're just setting out, it is much like a proposal your field sales team might prepare for one of its biggest prospects. But in this case, it's your own C-suite you are selling to, and as we all know, selling internally is often harder than selling externally.

A charter also helps you keep your discipline on track. Sales force enablement professionals function in a constantly changing environment and are bombarded with requests to shift priorities and add new projects to their to-do lists. When this happens, you can use your charter as a guide to determine your best course of action. As we talk about challenging situations in future chapters, you'll find us referring to the charter again and again. We can't stress enough how much a charter can help you overcome many of the obstacles you'll encounter.

As proof of the difference having a charter makes, we can refer to the *CSO Insights 2017 Sales Enablement Optimization Study*. Only 35% of organizations with a random or informal sales enablement structure felt that their sales enablement efforts met or exceeded expectations. That percentage jumped to 51% for organizations that had a formal sales enablement charter (see Figure 4.1 and also see Figure I.1). No doubt, this is due in part to the structure a charter provides, but the process of creating

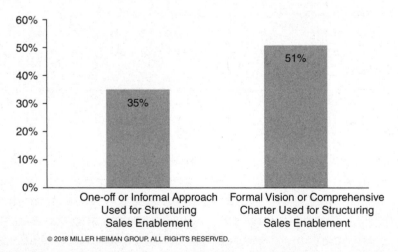

Figure 4.1 Initiatives Meeting All or the Majority of Expectations as Related to Sales Enablement Function Structure

a charter is also an important exercise in setting expectations appropriately, as we'll discuss.

> Your charter functions as your business plan and is your guide for turning a random sales enablement effort into a formal, scalable and strategic sales force enablement discipline that has a definable, positive impact on the business.

In this chapter, we will focus on the elements that should be included in your charter and how to start setting yours up. We'll refer you to later chapters for more detailed analyses and information, such as when we touch on the topic of goal setting. For now, we recommend setting up the structure of your charter and beginning the research required. Later, as we flesh out some of these concepts, you can come back to your draft charter and fill in the details.

Doing Your Research

The first step to creating an effective charter is to do your homework. As with any research, your initial purpose is to see enablement through the eyes of others, not to convince others of the rightness of your position. Try to go into this phase like an explorer, without any preconceived notions of what you'll discover.

Here are some of the best practices we've gleaned from organizations with a successful sales force enablement discipline.

Meet with executive leadership. Seek to understand the goals of the organization – not just specific sales goals but also vision goals, e.g., market share, expansion, new markets, etc. This is the audience your charter must convince, and stating your strategy and objectives in terms that are relevant to senior leadership will go a long way toward gaining buy-in and funding.

Meet with other departmental leaders, e.g., marketing, product management, HR, L&D, finance, IT, etc. In most organizations, these departments are already doing some sort of sales enablement, at least on an ad hoc basis. Find out what they are doing and what they think they could do with the right programs and processes in place. Many of these departments may see themselves as being at least partially responsible for sales enablement and will have questions as to how they fit into your broader plan. Remember, your goal at this point is to gather information, not to provide strategy statements that you may have to negate later.

Above all, look for ways that you can collaborate with these other departments to improve the process and demonstrate that you value their opinions and insights. As we'll discuss in Chapter 9 when we talk about cross-functional collaboration, sales force enablement does not and cannot be responsible for creating every enablement service. Including other team leads at this stage will help engender a spirit of conscious collaboration instead of competition.

Find a champion. From your initial discussions, a champion may emerge. Ideally, this champion will be someone from the C-suite who believes in sales force enablement as a discipline and is willing to help you overcome any obstacles or naysayers. If you don't have a champion or are unfamiliar with the concept, talk to one or two of your best salespeople to learn how they identify and work with a champion in their most important accounts.

Take stock of all random enablement initiatives. Enablement happens, even in organizations at the random enablement level. You should learn about some of the more conscious efforts by talking to the department heads, but also look for the one-off, spur-of-the-moment efforts. This includes all the random requests from sales to another department for assistance with something, such as technical information on a specific product, tweaks to a presentation and even requests for a meeting with a customer. Usually, these go through informal channels like email or phone and are never tracked, so the only way to get this information is to ask.

Random enablement also includes the efforts made by sales professionals themselves. In what areas do they spend time brushing up on their skills or knowledge, even if they have to track down the information themselves? Also, what content do they spend time creating? In the CSO *Insights 2017 Sales Enablement Optimization Study*, sales professionals created 18% of the content they used. Find out why they felt they had to create that content instead of using content that was already available. Finally, what processes and behaviors have they developed on their own that help them get more done in less time?

Managing Multiple Priorities

The ability to manage multiple priorities is the hallmark of an effective leader and an effective team. As you do your research, no doubt you will encounter multiple opinions on the purpose of sales enablement and what its goals should be. The CSO *Insights 2017 Sales Enablement Optimization Study* examined the top performance (see Figure 4.2) and productivity goals (see Figure 4.3) for sales enablement.

Many of these goals compete against each other for time and resources. Focusing on one can mean missing other targets. For example, new account acquisition is one of the most expensive ways to increase revenues. If enablement is asked to focus simultaneously on "increase in new account acquisition" and on "reduction in cost of sales," the team may find achieving these objectives doubly challenging.

While the research phase isn't the time to commit to any specific goals, eventually you will need to find a way to balance and prioritize competing goals and gain buy-in for your decisions. This starts by determining your goals based on your business and sales strategies.

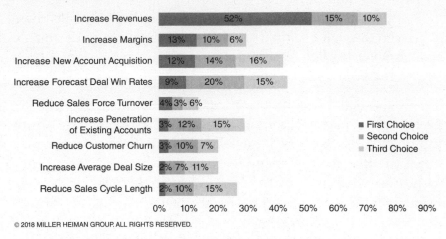

Figure 4.2 Top Sales Performance Goals

Business strategy: The goals of the business tell you what's important to the organization. To garner support and funding for the enablement discipline, it is essential that your end goal be in support of those objectives.

Sales strategy: The sales strategy tells you how the organization expects to achieve its sales goals, and your enablement strategy must be aligned to it. For example, if an organizational goal is to enter a new market by selling

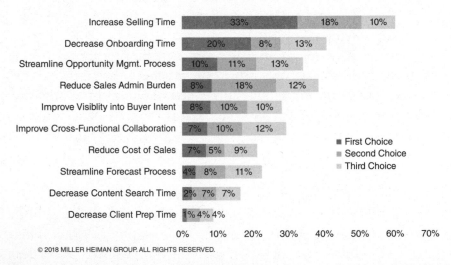

Figure 4.3 Top Sales Productivity Goals

exclusively through an indirect channel, your enablement efforts must align accordingly. You may agree or disagree with this approach, but that decision is outside of your control. Your role is to determine how sales enablement can effectively support the implementation of the sales strategy.

Create a Realistic Roadmap

Understanding the organization's business and sales strategy can help you create a vision for your enablement discipline and set priorities. However, you need to be realistic and consider another very important dimension that affects what your enablement charter, and specifically your roadmap, looks like: *enablement maturity*.

We've separated enablement maturity into four levels: Random, Organized, Scalable and Adaptive (see Figure 4.4). These four levels correspond to the CSO Insights Maturity Scale that we introduced in Chapter 1 – the maturity scale designations are in parenthesis – however, we've added a label for some of the levels in the sales force enablement maturity scale that reflects the importance of moving from one level to the next.

> *Random (Random)* – At this level, there is no discipline we could call sales enablement. Various functions claim to support sales. However, their services are created on an ad hoc basis, from a functional perspective. Furthermore, there is no consistency between services, and they are

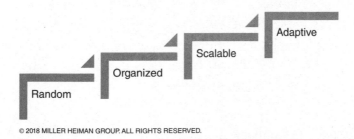

Figure 4.4 The Sales Enablement Maturity Model

thrown over the fence to sales with little guidance on how to use them and without any mechanisms to gather feedback.

Organized (Informal) – To have any impact on sales productivity and performance, the Organized level is the minimum level you need to achieve. At this stage, we would still consider this sales enablement (not sales *force* enablement yet) since your efforts are most likely targeted at one audience, usually field sales, and you may be more focused on one domain over another, such as content over training. At this level, the main objective is to organize whichever area you chose as your initial focus. This is your starting point, and there is no right or wrong place to begin. To have any impact on sales productivity and performance, the Organized level is the minimum level you need to achieve.

Scalable (Formal) – At the Scalable level, your discipline has matured into sales force enablement because you've targeted all sales roles, including sales managers, and you may even have begun to enable other customer-facing team members. In addition, your services efforts are getting broader in scope, and you are developing them in collaboration with other teams to build a scalable enablement engine. Customers are the main focus of all enablement services, but there will probably be situations where you need to revise services, such as product-focused content or training, contributed by other teams.

The Scalable level is the one represented in our definition of sales force enablement. For the most part, this is where we focus our discussion because the Scalable level is where you start to see real performance results.

Adaptive (Dynamic) – At the Adaptive level, you've developed a mature and highly adaptive sales force enablement discipline, serving all customer-facing roles and their managers. You're even offering enablement services to your service professionals. Your services are tightly tied to the strategic objectives of the organization and mapped to your internal processes. They are produced through the orchestration of efforts from multiple teams, with customers as the design point, right from the beginning. You may not be perfect, but you are World-Class.

Even if you've been given carte blanche to set up an enablement discipline (which rarely happens), maturing that discipline to Scalable levels, and eventually Adaptive levels, takes time. The types of goals you set will be different at each stage, from milestone goals as you're first setting up your discipline, to productivity goals as things get going, to performance goals as the discipline reaches a more mature stage. We will discuss these types of goals in greater detail in Chapter 12 when we focus on specific metrics. For now, as you set up your charter, we recommend focusing on doing your due diligence around the first three factors of business strategy, sales strategy and the current state of sales execution.

After Major Acquisition, Enablement Helps Combined Organization Reach Growth Objectives

In May of 2015, Cable & Wireless acquired one of its main competitors, precipitating a significant overhaul of its organizational structure and operating model aimed at taking what was a set of rather lumbering, underperforming assets and turning them into a cohesive, growth-oriented company. One of the main changes was a shift from a country-centric model – as a combined entity, Cable & Wireless operates in about 24 countries in total – to one that was oriented to the primary customer segments of residential, B2B and wholesale.

With that as a backdrop, the newly appointed president of the B2B organization set out six strategic imperatives, one of which was to build and develop a premier sales organization. Quite simply, the only way to meet investors' growth expectations was to ensure that the company had the most talented, skilled and successful sales organization in the business.

According to Boris Kluck, VP of Sales Operations for the combined organization, "Given that we were bringing two companies together with very different organization models and structures, and as you might imagine, a completely fragmented set of sales strategies, methodologies, processes and the like, it was important to make a big investment in sales enablement as a foundational element in being able to achieve those growth ambitions."

The sales organization set out to achieve a number of ambitious objectives:

- Improve overall sales results and productivity.
- Dramatically improve each salesperson's performance to quota.
- Ensure sales professionals maximized selling time with clients.
- Drive efficiency by improving win rates and conversion rates.
- Relentlessly focus on delivering a superior customer experience throughout the sales process.

"At the time we started our journey, not only were we not focused on any of the above in any sort of methodical and cohesive way, we had no measurement systems in place. So, even if we were trying to achieve those goals, we would have had no idea if we were being successful," says Kluck.

To address the challenge, the Cable & Wireless enablement team took a three-step approach:

Step 1: Define Enablement

To effectively collaborate across disparate teams, Cable & Wireless's new combined sales organization had to first define what they meant by "enablement." Ultimately, the scope of the discipline included several elements such as:

- The way the sales organization collaborates and engages with other functional areas of the business.
- How technologies and systems can be leveraged to improve effectiveness and efficiency.
- The processes that underpin the end-to-end sales cycle and result in predictable and consistent outcomes.
- A continuum of enablement services, such as talent management, rewards and recognition, business metrics and reporting, and performance management.

Step 2: Gain Stakeholder Buy-in

Fortunately, the business unit president was extremely supportive of the sales enablement agenda and went as far as enshrining the mandate of building and developing a premier sales organization as one of his six strategic imperatives. Having this top-down support helped remove any barriers or objections to the various initiatives implemented by the enablement organization.

Step 3: Secure Stakeholder Engagement

Stakeholder buy-in was important, but the team also needed stakeholders to contribute. While they had some pretty clear ideas of what they wanted to accomplish, enablement needed to ensure that a wide cross-section of key stakeholders from various departments and levels within the organization were engaged in the design and deployment of enablement services.

"By being part of the process, we found that it became easier to overcome any reticence those groups might have had if we had just tried to force our agenda," adds Kluck.

Pulling It All Together

Now, it's time to begin pulling everything together into a charter you will present to senior leadership. This chapter is only the beginning. We'll start by defining the four primary sections your charter needs to include. Then, in subsequent chapters, as we discuss each of the middle facets in more detail, we'll provide guidance on how to go back and update your charter with important details.

In the appendix, we've included a sample charter you can use as a guide. However, it is only a guide. Your charter will be as unique as your business context. Feel free to adapt what we offer to a style and level of detail that meets your needs.

Section 1: Situation. In this section you set the stage for everything to come by describing the context of your organization based on your initial research. As we described above, business strategy comes first because your goals must be aligned to the goals of the organization. Go-to-customer strategy comes next because this is how the sales organization is expected to achieve the organizational goals. Finally, you need to have a short section describing current sales execution so that the reader has a picture of where you're starting from. In our sample charter, we've also included reference documents in this section so that the reader understands the basis on which you're making your claims.

Section 2: Success. In this section, you go deeper into the details of your enablement plan and define what success looks like.

Vision describes the future state of the enabled sales force. Generally, this section is more aspirational in nature, painting the big picture for the reader.

Mission describes how you will reach your aspirational goals. It's more specific than the aspirational vision statement, but save the details for later. At this point, you just want to describe your approach.

Objectives describes what you want to achieve. This section tells the reader where you are going to place your emphasis. For example, an organization with high turnover might emphasize decreasing new-hire ramp-up time, whereas another organization with longer than normal sales cycles might emphasize a decrease in the time its opportunities spend at a specific stage. At this point, you don't need to apply a time parameter to these objectives as you will cover that in the roadmap section.

Metrics describes what success looks like. How you measure progress will vary according to your enablement maturity stage, but the metrics you include in the charter are the ones you are seeking to ultimately influence. You'll notice that most of the metrics examples we have in our sample charter (see Appendix) are different from the metrics sales uses to measure success. You need to select metrics you can impact directly that *lead* to performance improvements.

Section 3: Scope. Here's where you define your target audiences. Like objectives, there is no time parameter. Even if you decide to just start out enabling the field sales role in one region, you will want to highlight the other roles and regions that you plan to enable as your discipline matures.

If you sell through an indirect channel, you will want to enable internal channel personnel, too. You may also want to prioritize enablement services for your indirect channel partners. This is one of those areas where doing your homework pays dividends. Organizations and individual leaders hold different opinions on how much indirect channel enablement they should be responsible for. Before you prioritize the channel, be sure you understand the prevailing viewpoint in your organization. Don't be surprised if there isn't a consensus and you start a round of impassioned debates.

Finally, sales managers play an incredibly important role in the adoption and reinforcement of enablement services, and they require additional enablement services to help them coach salespeople in their day-to-day activities. While they may not be your first target audience, remember to include them in your overall plan. It's encouraging to see that sales managers are the second most targeted audience in the CSO Insights 2017 study, but at 68%, it's clear many organizations still have work to do.

Section 4: Roadmap. This section is critical as it helps set expectations for what you can achieve and by when, and it is highly connected to your enablement maturity level. We will get into more detail on defining your road map based on your enablement maturity level in a later chapter, but for now, you can just familiarize yourself with the sample we've provided.

"You have to have a charter to get everyone on the same page. And you need to get executive buy-in. Based on the interviews and audits we did, we put together an ROI-based business case to show the investments and the results we were aiming for. This business case supported our enablement charter. Make it practical and tangible for your senior executives. Show them what, for instance, a piece of content costs to be designed, created, localized, provided and maintained and the impact of creating enablement services that are not used. Then show them how you spend money and save money at the same time by focusing only on what's really required. This way you show them how you support their business strategy by enabling the sales force to achieve their goals. Our announcement came from our executive leader: This is what we are doing, why we are doing it this way, and this is what's happening next. And it was adopted."

Christine Dorrion, CallidusCloud,
VP Global Sales & Channel
Operations and Enablement

Prioritizing Your Enablement Efforts

In many organizations, sales force enablement professionals are bombarded with requests for various services. Some, such as content that can be used to sell to a specific market segment, come from the sales team. Other requests come from outside of sales, such as a request from product management for training materials for a new product launch. These are just two examples. No doubt, you've got an inbox full of similar requests right now.

The only way to sort through these requests and your own ideas, prioritize the important ones and eliminate the unimportant is to assess them in terms of the customer's path and your enablement charter. What does your salesperson need to help customers move forward in their buying process, feel comfortable about doing business with your company and implement their chosen solution to reach their targeted goals? At a higher level, which requests help you reach the goals you set out to obtain in your charter? That might be a training course on a new product. It might be a piece of content. It might be a package of services designed to support a new product launch.

Whatever the answer, a formal sales force enablement charter can help you arrive at the right decision. Individual salespeople (and other stakeholders) might not always agree with the decisions you make, but if you can justify your enablement priorities in light of the customer's path and your enablement charter, it's hard to argue with your choices.

Questions to Consider

- How well have we made the business case for enablement?
- What gaps do we need to address in our current enablement charter?
- Who are the key executives from whom we still need to gain buy-in? Who are the important influencers in our "sale"? Is there anyone we've overlooked in the past?
- What additional research do we need to do before we can create an effective charter?

Immediate Actions

Jot down two or three actions you will take to start preparing your enablement charter or to improve your existing one.

PART

III

Enablement Services

IN PART TWO, we laid out the importance of using a framework as a guide to building a holistic, effective sales force enablement discipline, and we took you on a quick tour of the Sales Force Enablement Clarity Model. Then, we looked deeper at three fundamental aspects of the clarity model: the importance of doing everything with the customer in mind, the concept of focusing your efforts on customer-facing professionals and their managers, and the need for creating a comprehensive charter to get executive buy-in for your strategy.

In Part Three, we're going to focus entirely on enablement services. This is what enablement *does* (see Figure III.1). Everything else we've discussed so far has been leading up to enablement services, and almost everything we will talk about in future chapters will be in support of them. Enablement services are how the discipline enables sales. Furthermore, as most of what enablement does is behind the scenes, services are the only thing your target audiences ever see.

Figure III.1 The Sales Force Enablement Clarity Model

Why Do We Call Them Services?

We chose this term, instead of another term such as "deliverables" or "output," to emphasize that enablement is something you *do and provide for others*. Speaking in terms of a deliverable or output focuses the conversation on the end product, whereas sales force enablement is responsible for the entire process: strategy, definition, creation, localization, publishing, delivery, and implementation and adoption of services.

We also chose not to use "programs," another common term because it carries various connotations in the minds of sales and enablement professionals. For example, some see programs as another word for training. Others see programs as having a more project-oriented focus. Enablement is clearly much more than training and more than just another one-off project. It is a discipline, with services as the method for achieving the goals that have been defined in the enablement charter.

Finally, we chose services to emphasize that sales enablement's reason for being is to deliver value to its target audiences so they, in turn, can deliver value to their customers. Sales force enablement does not exist for its own sake. It is a service-oriented discipline focused on a specific set of internal customers as defined in the charter.

> Sales force enablement does not exist for its own sake. It is a service-oriented discipline focused on a specific set of internal customers as defined in the charter.

Three Categories of Services

We break services down into three main categories: content, training and coaching. In the next three chapters, we will discuss the scope of each of these types of services and look at how they impact sales productivity and performance.

While each of these services has its own chapter, in a mature enablement discipline, none of these services stands alone. As we often tell our clients: *There is no content without training, and there is no training without content.* That is, all content services require some training to enable the sales team to use them effectively. For example, if enablement produces a playbook, sales will need training to learn how to effectively use it. That might be a short video training to familiarize them with the materials. Or, for a playbook designed for a new market or a new product line, it could be a multi-day workshop complete with role plays. Likewise, all training services require foundational training content such as presentations, worksheets and quizzes.

In turn, both content and training services require coaching to ensure the services are implemented and adopted appropriately. Coaching services provide sales managers with the content, tools and training they need to successfully coach sales professionals in their day-to-day activities. In the case of coaching services, the principle of no content without training, and no training without content is embedded in each and every coaching service.

As you begin to build your enablement discipline, you may focus more on one set of services than another. For most organizations, the initial focus will be on either content or training. However, as your enablement discipline matures, you'll broaden your scope and tighten the alignment between services. It's important to begin with this aligned vision in mind, even if you aren't there yet. We'll end our coverage of enablement services with a discussion on the role of value messaging in creating consistency between services.

5

Content Services

Key Points

- Content includes both customer-facing (external) and enablement (internal) assets.
- Not all content is "marketing content," and sales still creates too much on their own.
- The purpose served by content differs for each phase of the customer's path.
- Enablement needs to fulfill its role as orchestrator to ensure relevant content is created for every phase of the customer's path.

The Role and Scope of Content in Enablement

Salespeople move up the relationship spectrum by adding valuable perspectives during every interaction with prospects and customers. But not every interaction is verbal or even face-to-face. Offering the right piece of *customer-facing content*, such as a case study or white paper, at the right time can keep the value flowing even when the salesperson isn't sitting directly across from the prospect.

Content can also be used to build the salesperson's skills and knowledge. *Enablement content* is any content designed to help customer-facing professionals prepare for interactions with prospects and customers. Examples include playbooks, battle cards, cost-justification tools and so on. This content could be context-specific, such as a discussion guide for selling equipment into the oil and gas market. Or, it could be a playbook that provides salespeople with an overview of what they need to know, links to related content and relevant value messages aligned to the customer's point of view. It might also be content, such as a product-launch presentation, that supports a broader enablement initiative.

"Content is a concept. I'm finding 'situation-ready content' clarifies for everyone. It focuses everyone on the right question—content for what purpose, for what situation."

Jim Burns, President, Avitage

To be successful at helping customers move forward, salespeople need enablement and customer-facing content for each phase of the customer's path (see Figure 5.1). To help illustrate the scope of content that is needed, we'll introduce the enablement services framework in this chapter. In the next two chapters, we

Figure 5.1 The Sales Enablement Services Framework Part 1

will build this framework out as we talk about training and coaching services.

At the top of the enablement services framework, we have the customer's path. Again, we know that there is not one single customer's path; the details are different for every buying team and every scenario. Beneath the three phases are the goals sales must achieve for customers to move forward. We covered this in detail in Chapter 4, but let's review these again, adding more detail on the types of content needed at each phase.

> To be successful at helping customers move forward, salespeople need enablement and customer-facing content for each phase of the customer's path.

In the Awareness phase, salespeople need to help buyers create a future vision of success. Without this future vision of success, the customer cannot move to the buying phase and the deal stalls. Buyers need high-level content that helps them better understand their challenges and how to solve them. White papers (written from a business perspective and not a technical one) and case studies are two primary examples of awareness-phase, customer-facing content. Shorter-form content such as blog posts and articles are also valuable. If you'll remember from our discussion in Chapter 4, salespeople need plenty of this type of content because it is what they use to engage prospects and customers through social media.

Enablement content at this phase is designed to help the salesperson create a shared vision of a better future state so the customer can move on to the buying stage. Salespeople also need to be enabled to engage customers earlier in the awareness phase as it's always easy to create a vision of a better future state before the buying team has been overly influenced by competition, industry influencers or peers. Enablement content for this phase might include industry playbooks that help the salesperson understand the market landscape, the challenges of the industry, the various buyer roles and their pain points and so on.

Social media guidelines highlighting which materials to share, with which audiences and when can help the salesperson engage buyers before they are ready to talk to sales. Enablement content could also include higher-level guidelines designed to build a salesperson's skills, such as a guide for effectively using LinkedIn.

Once buyers move to the Buying phase, the salesperson's goal becomes one of helping them make the best decision from among multiple options. At this phase, customers are no longer interested in a high-level view of what the solution means to them. They have a vision, and now they want to understand how to achieve that vision in their organizations. This requires the sales professional to add a deeper level of perspective, mapped to the customer's context and desired results.

Customer-facing case studies, white papers, articles and posts are still appropriate, but salespeople need to share those that are focused on this particular buying team's vision. Financial buyers on the team will be looking more closely at the financial aspects of the solution, so the content offered needs to include a financial benefit. The technical buyers on the team may also be taking more of a role, and they will require more technical content to satisfy their information demands.

In 2016, our research showed that 61% of buying teams require an ROI analysis before they make a decision, so cost justification tools are an excellent example of enablement content needed in the buying phase. Salespeople may need content that guides them on the best way to handle objections, overcome a competitor's positioning and answer more technical questions. They will also need proposal templates, service level agreement (SLA) attachments and the other types of content required to close a sale.

"I consider anything related to enabling the sales team to have the right conversation with the right buyers at the right time to be content. This can be content like white papers, solution guides, implementation guides, success stories, third-party research. Internal content includes content like a sales playbook, competitive overview, positioning guide, sales process and also tools like ROI calculators, win-loss calculator etc.

"[Customer-facing content] must be aligned to the customer language, industry and environment. It is important to identify the key stakeholders, their role in the organization and the business problems they try to solve. It is important to realize there is no one size fits all. It must be aligned to the individual and sometimes even to the specific opportunity."

Thierry van Herwijnen, Sales Enablement Leader, Host of The Sales Enablement Lab

In the Implementation and Adoption phase, the salesperson ensures that the value sold gets delivered and then communicated to the stakeholders. The goal here is not only to ensure customer satisfaction, but to uncover opportunities to add additional value. In many ways, the customer-facing content in this phase is similar to the customer-facing content needed in the awareness phase because, as new opportunities are uncovered, the customer is embarking on a new customer's path. In addition, content such as tips and tricks, articles on how to drive adoption and other supporting materials can add value during the implementation and adoption phase. Content that highlights the benefits of renewal is also important in many industries.

Internal enablement content plays an even more important role because many salespeople are not taught to manage opportunities and entire accounts during the implementation and adoption. Guidelines for overcoming common trouble spots or how to coach customers through the sometimes long process of implementing a solution can be of tremendous help. Many salespeople also need guidelines for asking questions that help uncover the value delivered, tools that help them calculate the actual business value and presentation/report templates that help them communicate that specific business value back to the customer.

The examples we've shared just scratch the surface of what's needed in each phase (see Table 5.1). The types of customer-facing and enablement content needed vary based on the dynamics of your market and your organization. And of course, the specific pieces your salespeople share with their customers or use internally to prepare for an interaction with the customer need to be aligned to each buying team's unique path.

Enablement Spotlight: Social Selling

Back in the day, salespeople were often told they needed to be good at cold calling if they wanted to be successful. And if they couldn't be good at it, just do a lot of it, and the sheer volume of calls would make up for lack of skill. Some sarcastically named the technique "dialing for dollars," and very few salespeople enjoyed doing it.

Thankfully, social selling has replaced cold calling as a primary tool for sales success. Our 2017 study data showed that when social strategies are aligned across marketing and sales, win rates for forecast deals can improve by as much as 15%, and organizations with over 90% adoption rates for social strategies had an almost 20% improvement in quota attainment over those organizations with adoption rates of 25% or less.

Of all the tools salespeople cite, LinkedIn reigns supreme. To help their users improve their social selling acumen, LinkedIn created the Social Selling Index (SSI). The SSI scores a salesperson's LinkedIn activity against four pillars that are shown to drive higher performance. According to LinkedIn's analysis, those who score higher on the SSI have 45% more sales opportunities in their funnel and are 51% more likely to hit quota.

There are several ways sales force enablement can foster social engagement:

Table 5.1 Examples of Content Services

	Awareness	Buying	Implementation
Customer-facing content	■ Case studies ■ Success stories ■ White papers and thought leadership assets ■ Third-party research assets ■ Diagnostic tools ■ Business challenge oriented, and buyer role specific presentations	■ Proposal templates ■ Business value/ROI templates ■ Contract templates ■ Recorded or scripted product demonstrations ■ Case studies, references, testimonials ■ Product presentations and documentation ■ Collateral	■ Case studies ■ Implementation guidelines (tailored to industry and challenge) ■ Best practices implementation guidelines ■ Report to management templates (record progress)
Enablement content	■ Playbooks (can be crafted to cover all three phases) ■ Guided selling scripts ■ Ideal customer profiles ■ Funnel management tools ■ Training assets	■ Playbooks (can be crafted to cover all three phases) ■ Guided selling scripts ■ Battle cards ■ Opportunity planning tools ■ Training assets (see Chapter 6)	■ Playbooks (can be crafted to cover all three phases) ■ Guided selling scripts ■ Implementation checklists ■ Account management tools ■ Training assets ■ Relationship mapping templates

Tools: Many sales professionals have been using social engagement tools like LinkedIn and Twitter for years. Sales force enablement can help them be more effective by looking for complementary tools that help them analyze and manage their online engagement. Examples: Hootsuite, TweetDeck, Everyone Social, Buffer and Crowdfire.

Training: Social selling training must go way beyond tool training. Sales professionals need to understand not just how to use a tool like LinkedIn, but how to use it effectively. In our 2016 research, we found a correlation between effective social selling training services and performance. Win rates went up by seven points and quota attainment improved by six.

Content: The key to successful social engagement is to add value for the customer at each stage of the customer's path, especially during the awareness phase while the customer is still gathering information. The more value salespeople add, the more they stand out in a crowded marketplace and the earlier in the sales cycle they can engage the prospect. To do this, sales needs effective content. Sales force enablement can orchestrate content to ensure that sales has what they need.

"The challenge is feeding reps the right content. Curation. Your reps aren't going to be creators of content. Not very many of them. It's not their core skill set. I say OPC, Other People's Content. Whose content should they curate? The smarty-pants people in your buyer's world. Curate third-party thought leadership content. Share that content. Engage with that content. It's a great way for reps to become more visible on a topic of interest."

*Jill Rowley, Social Selling Evangelist
and Adviser, Chief Growth Officer at Marketo*

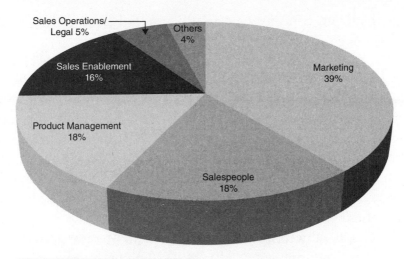

Figure 5.2 Sales Content Creation by Function

Who Creates Content?

A lot of sales enablement leaders don't pay enough attention to content services because in their minds "that's marketing's job." However, when CSO Insights asked the participants in its *2017 Sales Enablement Optimization Study* which functions create the content salespeople need for their selling efforts, the results painted a different picture.

Marketing creates only 39% of the content salespeople need for their selling efforts.

Marketing professionals may create some of the content sales uses, but they are usually not responsible for the entire content domain along the customer's path (see Figure 5.2). One way enablement leaders can permanently put to rest the misconception that all enablement content is created by marketing is to get rid of the term "marketing content." It's misleading and doesn't add any value to the discussion. Instead, label content according to its purpose or its intended audience. What sales needs is customer-facing content (externally focused) or enablement content (internally used), but not marketing content.

Product management (18%), sales operations/legal (6%) and other sources (4%) provide specific content for the buying and implementation and adoption phases.

Other teams, especially product management professionals, are strong contributors to content. Product management is needed for the detailed content required during the buying phase, such as technical presentations, recorded demonstrations, technical definitions and schematics. Content from product management is also crucial during the implementation and adoption phase as salespeople and other customer-facing professionals communicate the value delivered. Sales operations, legal and other teams contribute to other types of content, including proposal templates, service level agreements, and legal and contract attachments.

Enablement teams create 16% of the content salespeople need for their selling efforts.

Our clients are often surprised by this finding. Some expected a higher percentage; others thought it would be lower. Though enablement is often seen as the responsible role for many types of enablement content, such as playbooks, guided-selling scripts and value-justification tools, a lower percentage isn't necessarily a bad thing.

Content must be a collaborative effort. The special expertise required of sales force enablement is the ability to connect the knowledge salespeople and buyers need with their content consumption preferences and orchestrate contributions from other functions. Regardless of what percentage of content is seen as coming from enablement, the real question is: Is enablement effectively orchestrating the process?

Salespeople still create 18% of the content they need on their own.

While an improvement from 2016 (26%), this percentage is still too high because this is time the sales professional could spend adding value for customers. Whenever sales professionals have to create their content from scratch, something is wrong with the overall enablement approach. At most, salespeople should only have to tailor and customize content that has already been provided. If salespeople can't find the right content, aren't satisfied with its quality or don't know how to use the tools, then fixing these problems is enablement's responsibility.

"Our challenge is to enable the sales force as fast as possible, what the new offerings are, what problems they solve and what value they can create and what the right value messages for the relevant buyer roles are. To effectively respond to this challenge, we leverage the power of playbooks and sales kits so that our salespeople can find everything they need in one product or solution-based playbook."

Christine Dorrion, CallidusCloud,
VP Global Sales & Channel
Operations and Enablement

Content Services Need Work

As important as content is, it's surprising how poorly most organizations are doing in this area. There are two main challenges to overcome.

1. *Quality.* Only half (51%) of respondents in the 2017 study felt the quality of their content met or exceeded expectations. To be clear, when we say a piece of content isn't of sufficient quality, it doesn't always indicate shoddy workmanship. As often as not, it means that the content isn't effective in helping the customer move forward. For example, a customer story might be a well-written and well-designed piece of sales collateral, but if it fails to share tangible results or focus on the customer's challenge, it won't resonate with buyers and help them create a vision of future success.

2. *Quantity.* While we're firm believers in quality over quantity, slightly more than half (54%) of the respondents to the CSO Insights *2017 Sales Enablement Optimization Study* said the quantity of their content met or exceeded expectations. When they hear this, enablement professionals and other content creators often point to a repository full of assets and ask, "What more does the sales team want?"

While the sales team defines the issue as quantity, that may not be the issue at all. With limited resources, enablement often produces content that can be used broadly, such as across industries. What sales professionals want is content that can be used for their specific selling situation, such as content that addresses a specific issue or an industry need. They may also be referring to the lack of content that addresses a specific phase of the customer's path, such as a cost-justification tool that can be used in the buying phase.

While sales force enablement leaders should gather anecdotal feedback from their audience, they need to put that feedback in the proper perspective. The only metric that matters is whether the content is effective. And the only measure of effectiveness is whether it achieved the goal of helping prospects move to the next stage on their path, ideally faster than they would have without that content.

It's worth noting that there is a distinct difference between the perceived effectiveness of enablement content and customer-facing content. Content types that have an internal focus, such as product content, are ranked highly. For example, 53% of respondents rated their product collateral as meeting or exceeding expectations, with 48% naming technical/product presentations as a strength. On the other hand, the content types voted to be in most need of improvement included some highly critical customer-oriented assets: case studies, client-focused presentations and ROI templates (see Figure 5.3). We'll see this same sort of distinction in Chapter 6 when we look at the effectiveness of training services.

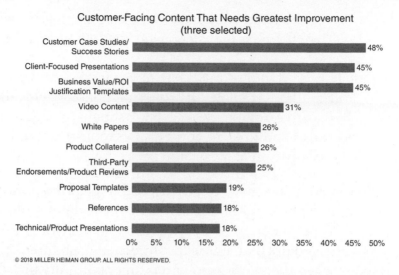

Customer-Facing Content That Needs Greatest Improvement
(three selected)

- Customer Case Studies/Success Stories: 48%
- Client-Focused Presentations: 45%
- Business Value/ROI Justification Templates: 45%
- Video Content: 31%
- White Papers: 26%
- Product Collateral: 26%
- Third-Party Endorsements/Product Reviews: 25%
- Proposal Templates: 19%
- References: 18%
- Technical/Product Presentations: 18%

Figure 5.3 Customer-Facing Content Types That Need the Greatest Improvement

Enablement Spotlight: Playbooks—A One-Stop Shop for Content

For an enablement professional, there is nothing more frustrating than creating a great piece of content that no one uses. Often the reason isn't because of the quality of the content or its fit-for-purpose; it's because salespeople simply can't find it fast enough when they need it. Playbooks can help ensure the right content gets in the hands of the salespeople at just the right time.

Designing your playbooks with a few best practices in mind can ensure maximum effectiveness—and usage.

Best practice #1: Create playbooks from a customer's perspective. Playbooks are internal enablement tools, but they should still be designed using a customer-oriented approach. Instead of creating product playbooks, create playbooks that correspond to a customer's business challenge or industry.

Best practice #2: Align your playbooks to the customer's path. No matter what the focus of your playbook is, every playbook should be aligned to the customer's path, with sections for what the salesperson needs to know at each phase.

Best practice #3: Use playbooks to reinforce your methodologies. For example, if your methodology includes Perspective Selling, the playbook should provide value messages and links to content and tools that can help the salesperson add valuable perspectives.

Playbooks do not have to be designed to be printed by the salesperson. They can just as easily take the form of an interactive PDF, presentation or website. More recently, the trend is to create modules that automatically generate an interactive playbook when the salesperson enters an opportunity into the CRM system. Additional modules may be added as customers progress along their path and the salesperson enters additional details about the customers' context, challenges and future-state vision.

Regardless of the form your playbook takes, aligning it to the customer's path and integrating your methodologies are essential. Let's take a high-level look at the types of content you might find in an industry-specific playbook.

Industry Playbook Outline

Section 1: Background Information	Market opportunity—Including segmentation details if the industry can be broken down.
	Competitive landscape—Who are the primary competitors? What are their strengths and weaknesses?
	Market dynamics—What macro and micro forces are driving the industry and impacting the prospect's business?
	Links to additional content such as industry forums and association sites.
	Glossary of terms and industry acronyms.

Section 2: Awareness Phase	Roles—Who is likely to be involved in an opportunity? What are their core business objectives and how are they likely to see the situation differently from other buyers on the team?
	Phase-specific value messages. Value messages can also be linked to specific roles.
	Methodology-specific content for this phase such as how to conduct a discovery with a potential prospect.
	Methodology and skills-related content, such as how to effectively engage potential buyers from this industry on social media.
	Links to awareness phase content, especially content that can be curated on social media.
	Links to phase-specific selling tools.
Section 3: Buying Phase	Phase-specific value messages. More detailed than in the awareness phase. Focus on business value and differentiation.
	Answers to commonly asked questions—may be role-specific.
	Links to more detailed content, such as technical schematics or white papers.
	How to overcome common objections. (Include any methodology-specific techniques.)
	Links to evidence of other customers who have achieved similar goals.
	Links to ROI tools or best-practice advice for how to create a cost justification for a company in this industry.
	Guidance on how to create a proposal for this industry and messages to use and/or links to proposal-building tools.

	Links to additional content and tools needed at this phase such as SLAs and contracts.
Section 4: Implementation and Adoption Phase	Methodology-based guidance on the role of the salesperson after the sale and how to have a value discussion in this phase.
	Role-specific questions designed to uncover delivered value and identify potential opportunities for adding future value.
	Worksheets for reporting and tracking value delivered.
	Links to proposal tools or contracts for renewals.

Orchestrating Content

In all but the smallest organizations, content is too big a job for sales force enablement to do on its own. Enablement's role is to orchestrate the contributions of other teams. Enablement is a logical focal point for orchestrating the process because they have the vantage point needed to gather input from sales, study the effectiveness of current content and identify gaps that must be filled. Plus, they don't have the role bias that other teams will have.

But orchestrating content is not easy. It requires balancing different work styles and managing multiple opinions on what type of content would be best. Here is a five-step process that can help you bring order to what can be a chaotic environment.

1. *Take stock of what you have.* Before creating new content, conduct an inventory of everything that is available, including any informal content, such as a presentation that was created by sales for a unique opportunity. If you're just starting out, this step can turn into a full-blown content assessment.

2. *Gather feedback and data.* You should be looking for feedback (and content) from several sources: customers, sales and internal teams that have contributed to past enablement efforts. In addition, you'll want to gather any data you have on the effectiveness of content. If you haven't yet invested in enablement technology, good data on which pieces move the customer through the funnel may be hard to come by. But even data on usage can be helpful at this stage. If one piece of content is frequently used and another hardly at all, you can ask for feedback from the sales team and customers on why they chose one and not the other.

Remember to gather feedback on gaps in content as well. Customers and salespeople will be able to tell you what content they don't have access to but would find useful. They may be getting this kind of content from third-party sources, such as analysts or their peers on social networking platforms. In that case, dig deeper into what purpose the content serves and whether it fulfills that purpose. Finally, ask the originators of the informal content why they created that content. All of this feedback will give you insights into the types of content you might need to create.

3. *Assess your assets.* Now that you have an inventory of your content assets and feedback from multiple sources, throw out any assets that are so obsolete they cannot be easily refreshed. Toss out redundant versions as well, and be brave about it. Having the same piece of content in multiple versions— without a valid reason for it—wastes resources, creates confusion and is difficult to maintain. Finally, using the feedback and data you gathered, identify those assets that are still relevant but need to be redesigned or improved.

4. *Identify the gaps.* Look for the gaps according to the phases of the customer's path, role, industry and so on, and then focus your efforts on creating new content or refreshing old content to fill those gaps. For example, the buyer roles may not be properly addressed (or not addressed at all), the industry may not be represented adequately, or the data points regarding

the business impact might need to be updated. If you're trying to transform your sales organization from product-centric to customer-centric, the content might be too focused on pitching product. The framework we introduced in this chapter can help you structure your content assessment and assure you look at each piece of content and its proper place along the customer's path.

5. *Prioritize*. In enablement, you can easily waste your energy on executing a multitude of activities that don't support your goals. It's essential to prioritize projects and activities based on an up-to-date charter that supports the current organizational and go-to-customer strategy. This allows you to focus your energy and create momentum in the proper direction. Those assets that are most closely linked to the objectives of the organization, especially those areas where performance needs to be improved, should be put at the top of the list.

Furthermore, enablement teams are bombarded every day with requests for this and that. A particular piece of content may sound like a good idea, but if it doesn't support the charter, it's a waste of effort. If your target audience insists that it is needed, it could be an indication your charter is out of date or isn't aligned as well to the goals of the organization as you thought it was. Whatever the reason is, enablement leaders should carefully assess all incoming requests to see whether they are in line with their charter. Of course, when prioritizing projects in a cross-functional discipline, differences of opinion can still arise. In Chapter 11, we'll talk about how an enablement advisory board can help you overcome these types of conflicts.

This process will help you see what you need to do to take your content efforts to the next level. If you're just starting out, the list of priorities is probably daunting. In Part Four, we'll look at how collaboration and a defined production process can help you get it all done efficiently and effectively.

Avoiding Sales Force Overload

Sales force overload—salespeople being pulled in too many directions—is a good sign that enablement is not orchestrating content effectively. In heavily siloed organizations, the problem isn't just a lack of collaboration. Teams often compete against each other to capture sales' attention. For example, product marketing may create training sessions, playbooks, brochures and other resources for sales in support of a product launch. At the same time, marketing decides to create a campaign to capture a larger percentage of more mature markets. Other teams also contribute to the battle for mindshare. For example, consulting may organize a boot camp for salespeople to teach them how to sell additional services along with their current product offerings.

Each of these initiatives may be valuable to the organization, but in this scenario, who could blame members of the sales team for complaining that they are being pulled in three different directions? By taking sales out of the field for training and spreading their time across three different initiatives, you increase the chance that all three will fail and sales will suffer.

As orchestrator, sales enablement functions as the gatekeeper for demands on sales' time by ensuring that all campaigns support the overall sales objectives and that sales still has enough selling time to meet its targets. Finally, they can gather feedback on the content's value to the sales team and use that information to orchestrate and improve efforts even further.

If you're seeing one or both issues crop up, you might be abdicating your role as orchestrator. Or, there might be a chance that you aren't getting the proper support from the department heads. Again, a formal collaboration model and an enablement advisory board (subjects we'll cover in Part Four) can help you overcome these challenges.

Your Next Steps

In this chapter, we talked about what enablement services are, focusing on content services. In Part Four, we'll fill in some of the details around the process of orchestrating the production and delivery of content services by covering the topics of collaboration (Chapter 9), leveraging technology (Chapter 10), operations and governance (Chapter 11) and measuring success (Chapter 12).

For now, however, we recommend reading Chapter 6 (training services), Chapter 7 (coaching services) and Chapter 8 (value messaging) to gain a clearer understanding of the scope of these services and how all three types of services must be aligned through value messages to provide the consistency the sales team needs to be effective. Even if you decide to focus your early efforts on the content domain, knowing how content supports and is supported by these other services will help you create a clearer vision for future success.

Questions to Consider

- How effective are our current content services? How are we measuring this?
- From which audiences do we gather feedback effectively, and how can we get better at gathering feedback from all audiences?
- Are we offering content designed from the customer's path, or are we applying more inside-out, product-centered thinking?
- Which functions create content in our organization, and how is content management organized?
- How effective is the cross-functional collaboration between our content creators?

Immediate Actions

Jot down two or three immediate actions you should take to improve the quality and effectiveness of the content made available to sales.

6

Training Services

Key Points

- Training services need to cover knowledge, methodologies and skills.
- Newer technologies offer a wide variety of capabilities and modalities designed to engage the modern learner.
- While learning and development teams are often responsible for training, sales force enablement must orchestrate the cross-functional collaboration needed to create and deliver effective enablement services for the sales force.

The Role and Scope of Training in Enablement

In each of the last three years of our study, training topped the list of enablement services offered. Clearly, training is already seen as having an important role in enabling sales. However, sales training means different things to different people. To effectively enable sales, training needs to address three different requirements:

1. *Knowledge*. Product training falls under this category of training services, as do many other types of training such as
   sessions on industry or market. Even methodology training
   and social selling training can fall under knowledge when
   these services focus on the process or the tool, answering
   questions such as how to move a lead from a prospect to an
   opportunity in CRM or how to set up a profile in LinkedIn.
   Knowledge training is important, but enablement services
   can't stop there.

> *Methodology training connects the sales process to the customer's
> path.*

2. *Methodology*. Methodology training helps the sales professional understand what to do and why. To use our knowledge training example from above, it helps sales professionals
   develop the situational fluency to assess a customer's context
   and concepts of a solution so that they can add the valuable
   perspectives that help the buyer move from prospect to opportunity. Methodology training connects the sales process to the
   customer's path.
3. *Skills*. Skills training covers those capabilities that are needed
   to execute the methodology along the customer's path. This
   can be everything from basic skills such as active listening, to methodology skills such as how to ask questions to
   uncover pain points, to more specific skills such as how to
   effectively curate content and engage buyers on social media.
   Skills training allows the salesperson to apply knowledge and
   methodology training in the field.

In this chapter, we've added a layer to our Sales Enablement
Services Framework to show the alignment of training to the customer's path and to content (see Figure 6.1). Some types of training will not be directly aligned to a phase. For example, general
selling skills are relevant throughout the customer's path. However, the customer needs to remain the focus of the training.

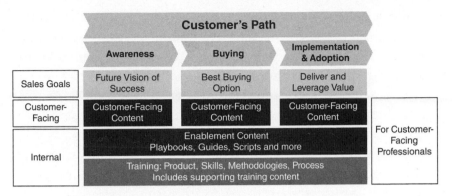

Figure 6.1 The Sales Enablement Services Framework Part 2

Sales Organization Sees 32% Pipeline Increase Within 60 Days When Content Is Combined with Training

What began as a training initiative for a multibillion-dollar organization quickly turned into a content project as well. It started when the organization decided it needed to standardize its sales methodology across the global sales team. To do this, it needed to teach that methodology to the entire organization in a way that was cost effective and stuck with the team even after the training was over. The company turned to Mereo, an independent revenue performance advisory firm that helps organizations drive consistent revenue performance.

When Jay Mitchell, President of Mereo, met with company managers, it was clear they had another problem as well. "They just couldn't get their salespeople to think about anything other than their products," says Mitchell. "One sales executive described how, on the way to a sales call, he would ask his salespeople to tell him about the business problem the customer needed to solve. Every single one of them launched into the features of the product they were trying to sell. They could not articulate any element of the use case the product was intended to solve."

Mitchell and his team started by conducting a series of fact-finding interviews with company managers, salespeople, subject matter experts and customers. "You have to get customers involved in the same meetings as the salespeople. They are the only people salespeople will really listen to. Sometimes, you need a customer to tell a salesperson to stop talking and start listening," Mitchell laughs, only half-joking.

In the end, Mereo did offer training to more than 300 salespeople over a three-month period, but the training was supported by more than three dozen playbooks segmented by competitor, industry, use cases and requirements such as regulatory compliance. Individually, each playbook was organized in line with the sales methodology, providing exactly the kinds of support the salesperson needed in order to follow the prescribed methodology yet adapt their specific approach to the customer's context.

The impact was significant and almost immediate. Following the implementation of the training program and playbooks, this organization saw a 32% increase in pipeline within 60 days, and the combined sales team went from 60 to 70% of quota to 110 to 120% of quota the following quarter.

Which Modality Is Best?

Despite the huge advancements in training technology and platforms, many organizations are still providing training in very traditional ways. When CSO Insights looked at which types of training are most frequently offered, nearly three-quarters of those surveyed selected on-site, classroom-based training. Webinar training was also popular as was "shadowing experienced salespeople," a traditional method with a long history in many companies. On-demand methods, especially mobile learning, were less common.

"We are a large company with over 300 sales professionals across 24 countries. The traditional face-to-face training methods just are not fit to scale across such an extensive organization, so we needed a more efficient and cost effective way to upskill our sales teams. Fortunately, we have had eLearning in place for over 10 years at Cable & Wireless and have an extensive library of programs. We mapped our sales competencies to programs in our eLearning platform and could identify courses, books and videos that could be used for the personal development for our sales professionals. To address individual development, managers were required to complete a development plan in collaboration with every team member."

Boris Kluck, VP Sales Operations,
Cable & Wireless Communications

"Road warriors" have been around for as long as there have been salespeople, but salespeople are more mobile than ever. They are also more connected, with smartphone, tablet and other device usage nearly ubiquitous in the sales profession. This level of connectivity makes it even more frustrating for the sales force to have to leave the field to attend a training session offered only in a traditional setting. M-learning (mobile learning) and e-learning training sessions can offer just-in-time training and refresher materials to salespeople when and where they need it.

Nevertheless, most salespeople tend to be people-oriented, and there is a benefit of getting them together to interact and learn from each other. Most of our clients use a combination of classroom-style learning and m-/e-learning modules to develop their salespeople. But even this classroom-style training is rapidly evolving to a more interactive approach and away from what some derisively call the "sage on the stage" approach where an instructor stands at the head of the classroom imparting knowledge.

In this new approach, m-/e-learning modules are used ahead of time to teach the concepts that the students then spend the majority of classroom time practicing and discussing. M-/e-learning modules are also used to reinforce the learning after the students leave the classroom and apply what they've learned in the field. Modern learning platforms also combine social media style capabilities with learning modules so that peer-to-peer interaction is not limited to the few times a year the sales force gets together face-to-face.

Reinforcement of learning through online modules and micro-reinforcement tools is essential. The forgetting curve, first introduced in the late 1800s and corroborated through additional research, shows that people will have forgotten an average of 50% of the information they just learned within one hour. Within 24 hours, they have forgotten an average of 70% of new information, and within a week, 90% of it has been wiped from their memory. Reinforcement training services can help students retain more information longer.

The Modern Learner

Technology is changing the way we gather information and learn new things at an increasingly rapid pace. Just a few years ago, if you needed to change the oil in your car and didn't know how to do it, you would have dug through the glove compartment for the manual, read the instructions the best you could, then given it your best shot. (Or given up and taken it to one of those instant oil-change places.) Now, a quick search on YouTube will serve up a video—and sometimes several— showing you exactly what to do, step by step, for your make and model of vehicle.

The ubiquity of handheld devices like smartphones also means we can learn wherever we are. In just the last five years, global penetration of smartphones has increased from less than 19% to nearly 75%. For many of us, Google and Bing are the go-to resource whenever we need to look something up, gather insights or learn something new.

This consumer-oriented approach to learning has affected the expectations we have for learning at work as well. We don't want to sit through hours of one-way lectures given by an instructor who can't relate to our experiences. We want to be empowered to set our own learning path and to learn from people (often our own peers) who clearly understand what it means to apply the learning in our role. When we need to learn how to do something specific, we want help to be as easily accessible and relevant to our circumstances as the oil-change videos on YouTube.

These new expectations aren't just restricted to Millennials or the iGen-ers (just beginning to enter the workforce) who seem like they were born with a smartphone in their hands. The reality of today's work environments means that everyone from the iGen to the oldest of the Baby Boomers is being asked to get more done in less time. With technology at virtually everyone's fingertips, workers in an increasing number of industries are developing what we call a "Millennial mindset" where they expect to be able to use technology at work to learn and gather information when and where they need it.

Let L&D Be Your Ally

If you've been offering product training sessions and little else, this chapter can leave you feeling a little overwhelmed. How can you possibly get from where you are today to where you need to be? If your organization has a formal Learning & Development (L&D) department or a training academy, you may be closer than you think. (If your organization does not have a formal L&D department, our section on orchestrating training found later in this chapter is one you'll want to pay close attention to.)

The makeup of L&D varies from organization to organization, but generally, these teams have at least one or two people who are experts/specialists in learning theory. Best case scenario, they have already invested in a modern learning platform that you can leverage. If not, it's likely that they have at least looked into modern learning platforms, but haven't been able to justify the investment to the business. You can provide them with the opportunity. Worst case, they have no idea what a modern learning platform is, and you can help them up their game while you investigate the opportunity together.

Once you are ready to begin developing training services, whether they are classroom services or m-/e-learning modules, you will need someone to lead the effort. Your L&D allies won't be the subject matter experts (SMEs), but they can help your SMEs translate their knowledge into useful enablement services.

If you don't have a background in training, getting up to speed on the terminology can help you have a more productive discussion with the learning professionals in your organization. Here are just a few terms with which you should be familiar:

Badging. Validations given to learners to attest to completion and passing of a course. Badges can be added to social profiles on platforms such as LinkedIn.

Credentialing. Similar to badging, credentialing is often used when attesting to the learner's competency in an area.

Gamification. Adds elements of game play to learning such as scoring points, leaderboards and badges. Since salespeople tend to be competitive by nature, gamification is particularly effective in sales force enablement.

LMS. Learning Management Systems. A somewhat outdated term that refers to the systems used to manage and maintain learning assets as well as data on attendance, course evaluations and student assessments.

Micro-learning. Learning that is delivered in short bursts that focus on a very specific topic. Generally, micro-learning is thought to increase retention. It also tends to be one of the best ways to increase participation within a time-strapped sales force.

M-learning. Mobile learning. Refers to learning assets that can be accessed through mobile devices.

MOOC. Massive Online Open Course—Originally offered by universities to the community, these online courses are open to anyone and free of charge. Private businesses are now taking the MOOC concept and transforming it into a learning platform for their sales organizations.

VILT. Virtual Instructor-Led Training. Training that is offered in a virtual environment where instructor and learner are in different locations. This type of training fosters interaction between instructor and learner, and sometimes, between learners.

Health Care Organization Uses MOOC to Provide Training to 1,600 Sales Professionals

In the past two years, IQVIA, an organization using insights, technology and intelligence to improve human health, has grown from 10,000 employees to over 50,000 worldwide. To grow the sales skills and capabilities within their 1,600 sales professionals working in a very complex and challenging environment, IQVIA needed to create training services that delivered on a number of goals:

- Build the skills of its global sales force efficiently and economically across multiple regions worldwide.
- Drive consistency in sales and CRM processes.
- Improve existing sales onboarding and retention practices.
- Increase cross-selling capabilities.
- Minimize time out of market for sales training.

To reach these goals, the team at IQVIA chose a blended learning MOOC-like approach.

The program, called "Progressing Your Sales Opportunities," centers on applied learning and real business outcomes using actual client business scenarios and opportunities. The course is primarily self-paced, with blended online and offline activities managed and delivered through the Intrepid Learning platform as well as an in-person peer and manager coaching component.

Using a modern learning platform from Intrepid allowed IQVIA to create a program that is scalable across multiple geographies and time zones with no limits to the number of learners who can use the system. Social capabilities, including discussion forums, commenting and "likes," increase engagement and interaction across the widely dispersed sales team. Gamification elements, such as a leaderboard, badges, best practice sharing, etc., fuel interest levels and competition. For the organization, the new approach eliminates the cost of bringing salespeople to a central location for training and minimizes time-out-of market for revenue producers.

Initial results are promising, and the program is now an integral part of IQVIA's new sales hires onboarding program. A three-month impact survey confirms that 81% of program participants are better able to align their clients' business needs to IQVIA's offerings and solutions, and their sales force is leveraging the power of networks through regular collaboration with peers. One hundred percent of IQVIA's sales managers use the manager tools provided on the platform, and more than 90% say they have already seen an improvement in their team's performance.

Enablement Spotlight: Onboarding New Hires

Onboarding new hires is an area where enablement can have a distinct and measurable impact with training. Given the high average turnover experienced by many sales organizations, a significant portion of the sales team is likely to be composed of brand-new and recently hired individuals. Our experience working with clients also tells us that new hires who are productive faster are less likely to leave the organization (voluntarily or involuntarily), taking all the invested time and effort with them. Therefore, it should come as no surprise that decreasing new hire time-to-full-productivity was the number two productivity goal cited by respondents to the CSO *Insights 2017 Sales*

Enablement Optimization Study, coming in right behind increasing selling time.

Calculating this potential impact of shortening the onboarding period for new hires and presenting it to senior leadership can help you cost-justify your enablement discipline. If you aren't sure what your average time-to-full-productivity is, here's a fast and easy way to measure it. First, list all the new salespeople hired in the past two years in column A of a spreadsheet. Then, in columns B through Y, enter their revenue contribution for each month since they came on board. Next, compare average new-hire performance to the average results from experienced sales professionals. At what point do your new hires start producing at the same level as your more experienced professionals? You can get much more sophisticated with the analysis, but this method should allow you to test your assumptions and calculate the potential impact of bringing new hires up to full productivity faster.

Orchestrating Training

These days, many organizations, especially larger ones and those selling more complex products and solutions, have L&D teams that are responsible for all training curriculum. When sales force enablement orchestrates the creation and delivery of training services for sales enablement, it isn't replacing the role of L&D; it is simply ensuring that training services meet the needs of the sales force.

The process you'll follow to organize your training efforts is much the same as the one we shared in our last chapter on content services. Let's look at these five steps again in the context of training.

1. *Take stock of what you have.* As with content, you need to first create an inventory of all the training services that are available to the sales force today. If training wasn't previously considered to be part of the enablement function, you may need

to search around a bit to see what's available. Get in touch with other departments, such as HR, L&D, marketing and sales operations, to see what, if anything, they offer. Official training sessions, such as product classes are easy to identify, but as with content, there may also be unofficial services you should include. For example, one of the product managers might have recorded an informal five-minute product demo and made it available to a handful of salespeople looking for more information. You'll need to dig down a layer or two to find these types of services, but ask around when talking to salespeople or other potential contributors.

2. *Gather feedback and data.* Salespeople and managers usually have plenty of feedback on which sessions are valuable and which sessions aren't—and why. This data, combined with course evaluations, gives you a baseline for assessing the perceived value of training services, but it doesn't always give a clear picture of actual value.

If you can correlate a training service to performance improvements, such as decreased cycle times, so much the better, but this may not be easy if you're just starting to develop your sales force enablement discipline. You often won't have systems to collect the granular data needed for a full analysis. However, you can compare data points like training assessments to overall performance levels. As with content, focus on the extremes, such as those with high assessments and high performance or low assessments and low performance, to gather insights into how training affects performance.

In the case of the informal training services you uncovered in step one, seek to understand why someone thought that training service was necessary. If product management thought it might be helpful, but sales never used it, that gives you a pretty good indication of its worth. On the other hand, if the request originated from sales, chances are it was intended to fill a sales need. Ask questions to learn more about that need.

Training is one of the ways forward-thinking employers attract and retain top talent. Successful salespeople look for companies that help them develop deeper, marketable skill sets.

Training is one of the ways forward-thinking employers attract and retain top talent. Successful salespeople look for companies that help them develop deeper, marketable skill sets. Lack of training is also one of the reasons successful salespeople leave the company. Exit interviews are an excellent time to gather feedback on the perceived effectiveness of your training programs. In fact, assessing why salespeople leave (voluntarily or involuntarily) is one of the top 12 World-Class best practices in our *2017 World Class Sales Practices Study*.

3. *Assess your assets*. Next, delete all assets from your list that are obsolete and cannot be easily refreshed. Since there are many types of training, you might also need to delete a few from your list that have nothing to do with sales enablement, such as many of the HR-mandated courses. Be careful about being too overzealous though. Some courses, such as ones on active listening skills, fit very well into sales force enablement and can be relatively easily adapted to make them even more impactful for customer-facing professionals.

4. *Identify the gaps*. Now, use the customer's path, your charter and the data and feedback you gathered to identify gaps in your training services. Here are some questions you might consider:
   - Which sales roles have we overlooked when creating training services? For example, if all your training is designed for your territory managers, you may need to create (or modify) services for those who sell into named accounts.
   - Which stages of the customer's path require additional training services? For example, during the implementation and adoption phase, are salespeople effectively selling the

value delivered? If not, what training services can help them learn this best practice?

- Which important skills are not being addressed with training? Newer skills, like social selling, are obvious examples, but it could also be a traditional skill such as negotiation.
- Which important skills need additional reinforcement? Even though you might offer training services for a particular skill, if the sales force isn't applying that skill, additional training services may be needed.

5. *Prioritize*. Just as with content, you're likely to be bombarded with constant requests for training services, both large and small. This is especially true in organizations that see training as synonymous—or nearly so—with enablement. If the organization still has a product-oriented mindset, many of these requests are likely to be geared toward products. Use what you've learned in this chapter and the charter you've created to carefully prioritize your efforts.

A Look Ahead

As with content, producing and delivering training services is a process that requires cross-functional collaboration. Training can sometimes even be more difficult as there can be many teams involved simultaneously, such as when you're hosting a sales kickoff conference comprising many sessions. We'll get deeper into the importance of the collaboration model and how to define your process when we talk about enablement operations in Chapter 11.

In the next chapter, we'll examine the third category of services: coaching. Coaching services include the training and content services that equip sales managers to be better sales managers, so they can reinforce knowledge, skill development and behavioral change as part of their daily work with sales professionals. While coaching services usually aren't an initial focal point for organizations just starting out on their enablement journey, they can have a significant impact on performance.

Questions to Consider

- Where are our current training services focused: Knowledge? Methodology? Skills? In which categories do we need to add or improve training services?
- How do we need to evolve our training services to leverage new technologies and meet the changing needs of our workforce?
- How can we better engage sales without taking them out of the field for training?
- How can we foster interaction between salespeople for peer-to-peer training?
- How can we better engage sales managers so they can reinforce training?
- How can our sales force enablement team do a better job of orchestrating training services?

Immediate Actions

Jot down two to three actions you should take to improve training services.

7

Coaching Services

Key Points

- Coaching services reinforce the content and training services provided to the sales team and improve the return on your investment in enabling salespeople.
- Effective coaching covers five key areas: lead and opportunity, funnel/pipeline, skills and behaviors, account, and territory.
- The most successful sales organizations enable their sales managers beyond just coaching.

Why Enablement Needs to Offer Coaching Services

First, let's level set on coaching. Sales coaching is the process by which sales managers and others use a defined approach and specific communication skills, combined with domain expertise, to facilitate conversations with team members to uncover improvement areas and opportunities for new levels of sales success.

On the surface, this is straightforward. Coaching has been a focus for selling organizations for decades. Unfortunately, most sales organizations we work with label coaching as one of their biggest challenges. Managers struggle with finding the time (and making the decision) to prioritize such conversations and they lack the methods, skills and tools for having such conversations consistently and effectively. Filling this gap will take a significant effort by the enablement organization and those with whom you collaborate.

Yet the payoff is powerful. Coaching is the best way to drive adoption and reinforcement of the initial investments in enabling salespeople. Developing coaching skills is also essential for an organization looking to make any sort of significant transformation, such as a move from a transactional, product-oriented approach to one focused on business outcomes.

In fact, the *2017 Sales Enablement Optimization Study* found that organizations that achieved *dynamic* coaching maturity by actively targeting sales managers with enablement services and purposefully driving coaching services aligned to an overall enablement framework could improve their win rates for forecast deals by 28% compared to the study's average of 52% (see Figure 7.1). If you are not there yet, you are not alone. Only 11% of

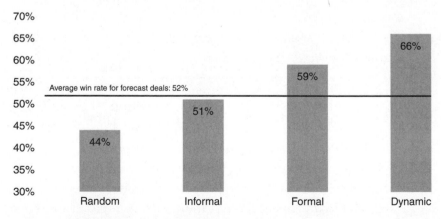

Figure 7.1 Sales Coaching Approach Impacts Win Rates for Forecast Deals

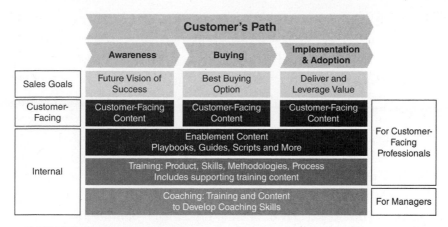

Figure 7.2 The Sales Enablement Services Framework Part 3

respondents had achieved this level of coaching maturity at this point in their enablement journey.

There is still much to be gained (14% improvement) from *formal* coaching maturity where you provide coaching training and hold people accountable for using it. Either formal or dynamic is preferable to an *informal* approach with a lightly documented approach and no reinforcement or accountability or worse yet, a *random* approach where coaching is left up to each manager to do as they see fit.

Coaching services add another layer to our enablement services framework and can help you move from random/informal to formal, and ultimately dynamic coaching maturity. Coaching services are content and training used to develop sales managers so they can coach their sales teams effectively, driving adoption and reinforcement of the initial enablement services provided for salespeople.

As you consider how to incorporate coaching services into your enablement framework (see Figure 7.2), be sure to think broadly about the audiences for these kinds of services. Most obviously, sales managers are the core target audience. However, they shouldn't be your only focus. Consider:

Salespeople themselves. Many tools, especially newer AI-enabled tools that synthesize data and surface insights, are designed to be self-service. For example, a diagnostic tool can use an analytics-driven definition of ideal customer criteria to assess an opportunity and recommend possible approaches and value messages to use. In those scenarios, salespeople will need to be enabled to use tools to analyze their own situations and coach themselves (ideally, in complement to the interactions with their sales managers).

Sales leaders and sales directors. Those who manage sales managers must be equipped for their roles in helping sales managers become more effective and leverage the methodologies, skills and tools they are provided. Coach-the-coach enablement services are an area for future growth for most organizations and enablement functions.

Coaches without administrative authority. Some organizations have professional sales coaches taking over, or supplementing, direct manager coaching. In others, there may be key leaders outside of the sales team who are in an appropriate position to coach salespeople effectively. Finally, you may implement peer coaching or mentoring programs. All of these individuals should be provided with the services needed to fulfill their coaching roles.

With an evidence-based case for why enablement should offer coaching services and for whom, we should discuss the end state, the types of coaching you will enable.

There Is More than One Type of Coaching

Most people think of coaching as conversations in which a manager and a seller consider what to do in order to close a specific piece of business. This is opportunity coaching, and it is assuredly important. Yet, it is only one of five different kinds of coaching that managers should be fully enabled for and executing on a

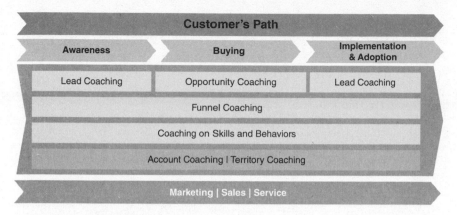

Figure 7.3 The Sales Coaching Framework

regular basis with each of their salespeople. In addition to opportunity coaching, effective coaches also focus on leads, the sales funnel or pipeline, skills and behaviors, account, and territory.

As we drill into the detail in order to highlight the differences among the five types of coaching (see Figure 7.3) and allow you to consider your own gaps and strengths, we mustn't forget the bigger picture. No matter what area coaches are discussing with a sales professional, they must always keep the customer as the focus of the conversation. For example, when discussing an opportunity, coach and salesperson aren't discussing sales techniques to move a customer from awareness to the buying phase. Instead, they are discussing how the salesperson can add relevance and differentiation so that the customer wants to move to the buying phase.

Lead and Opportunity Coaching

We talked earlier about the need to offer perspective and insights to customers and prospects early in the customer path, leveraging a detailed sales methodology for aligning the sales and buying processes. This is critical for organizations looking to climb the vertical axis in the SRP matrix because adding perspectives and insight are how salespeople add value for their customers. Furthermore, aligning the sales and buying process ensure this perspective and insight is offered at the right time.

> Coaching has the greatest impact when it starts in the early stages of the lead/opportunity. If the manager waits to coach until just before a deal is closed, the discussion may narrowly focus on approval for a discount.

Coaching to this end result has the greatest impact when it starts in the early stages of the lead/opportunity. If the manager waits to coach until just before a deal is closed, the discussion may narrowly focus on approval for a discount. This is neither coaching by our earlier definition nor does it drive relationship growth.

- In the initial stage, coaches should ask questions to help the sales professional identify the leads that are most likely to turn into qualified opportunities.
- Once opportunities are identified, the discussion turns to engagement strategies, leveraging relationships and how to tailor messaging. In the buying phase, coach and salesperson discuss where customers are along their path and how the sales professional can help them move forward. Note that opportunity coaching for every opportunity within a team may not be practical. Coaches should focus their efforts on opportunities that are stuck in the funnel or those that are must-win opportunities, strategic, high potential, etc.
- During the implementation and adoption phase, the focus turns back to lead coaching as the salesperson looks for additional ways to add value in existing accounts.

Sales enablement can support these kinds of coaching conversations by ensuring that coaches have mastered opportunity management methodologies and technology-enabled data analysis and planning tools and by providing detailed coaching guidelines.

Recommended Focus for Lead and Opportunity Coaching

- *Customer's business challenges and goals.* What is the actual problem, and what's the business impact of the issue? What are the desired results the customer wants to achieve, and how are the expectations different across the buying team, etc.
- *Customer context.* What is known about the customer and their buying process? How well does this opportunity match up to our ideal customer profile? What's their financial situation, what are the strategic initiatives?
- *Opportunity objective.* What is the solution and why will it help the customer? How will our solution be valuable, relevant and differentiating? What is the projected close date? What confidence level do we have?
- *Buying influences.* Who are the buying influences? What role do they play? How eager are they to act? What are their personal and organizational wins? What evidence do you have for these conclusions? Who and how will you engage to add perspective?
- *Situation analysis.* At this point in the process, what are your strengths and what may be working against you? What assumptions have you made? What is a risk or unknown?
- *Action planning.* What are the best actions you can take in order to leverage a strength or mitigate a risk? How will these actions help the customer make an informed decision? Does this merit additional resources? Are we internally aligned? When should we walk away?

Funnel or Pipeline Coaching

This area focuses on the structure of a salesperson's funnel or pipeline. Here, the sales manager works with the sales professional to help identify the most valuable deals that can be won and to manage risks and allocate resources accordingly. Funnel coaching also helps salespeople understand how the shape of their funnel translates into quota attainment and how they can best improve their funnel performance.

Sales force enablement can help by providing training and guidelines that help the coach better understand the science behind funnel management. Such training and guidelines can also develop sales managers' business acumen so they are better able to evaluate the risk/reward trade-off when evaluating opportunities and deciding where sales professionals should spend their time.

In this coaching area, close collaboration between sales operations and enablement is essential. Sales operations usually defines the funnel and forecast process. So, it is important that sales managers understand how their sales teams are expected to follow these processes and that they develop coaching skills to reinforce these behaviors. In addition, sales operations often has access to a larger set of data, often accessed via the CRM or integrated applications. Enablement can help coaches to access data and use it to understand not just whether salespeople are performing the right activities and reaching their targets, but also to identify the leading indicators of performance that show where salespeople might be challenged.

Recommended Focus for Funnel Coaching

- *Value and staging.* Are opportunities properly identified in the right stages? Does the staging align with the customer's path for purchase? How aligned are seller planned actions, customer commitments and stage identification? How accurate is forecasting based on staging?
- *Velocity.* What opportunities have moved? Why or why not? What is causing opportunities to get stuck? And what

should be done to improve flow? Have all verbal "yes" commitments been turned into formal closes? How does velocity compare to a high performer benchmark?

- *Volume*. Are there enough opportunities and leads to meet quota or other goals (product mix)? Which activities/ sources are most fruitful in filling the pipeline? What has fallen out of the pipeline and why? What are the appropriate next actions?
- *Shape*. Looking at the funnel overall, why is it shaped the way that it is? What are the biggest risks? What has changed? What needs to be done to have a more balanced funnel?
- *Time horizon*. It's a common pitfall to look at the pipeline for the next quarter or the current fiscal year. Depending on your average deal cycles (the longer, the more relevant it is), it's recommended to integrate different time horizons, such as for instance, 6 months, 9 months, 12 months and 18 months.
- *Action planning*. Where will you focus your selling time? What opportunities, leads and actions will you prioritize? How well does qualifying criteria help focus efforts?

Skills and Behaviors Coaching

Many of the actions that are identified in opportunity coaching involve conversations that the seller should have with the customer. The success of these conversations is predicated on the skills and behaviors of the seller: questioning techniques to surface needs that the customer was unaware of, presenting perspective in a way that enhances the customer's thinking, surfacing and resolving customer concerns. Perspective Selling is the method for acquiring, growing and retaining key customer relationships. Conversational skills are how those relationships take place, one interaction at a time.

Sales enablement supports this through deployment of selling skills to the frontline, developing coaches to a mastery level in these skills, providing support tools and training on how to role play critical sales conversations as well as technology-enabled call planning tools.

Recommended Focus for Skills and Behaviors Coaching

Ideally, coaching for skills and behaviors should take place after role plays or observing sales' interactions with customers and prospects—or after receiving a technology-enabled analysis of an interaction. Key skills that should be targeted in coaching sessions include:

- *Alignment to the customer's path:* How much was the conversation aligned to the customer's path? If not known yet, what steps were taken to identify the customer's current position along the customer's path? Given a certain stage of the customer's path, how relevant, valuable and differentiating was the interaction? Was is tailored and aligned or not?

- *Demonstration of value.* How did the customer benefit from the conversation? New perspective on what success looks like? New vision of solution possibilities? Expanded insights? Could we establish a shared vision of success?

- *Discovery of needs.* What proportion of time was the seller the speaker versus the customer? Use of open- versus closed-ended questions? Use of questions to help customer become aware of need? Impactful word choices? Use of silence?

- *Delivery of key messages.* How did sellers convey key value messages and how relevant were they to the customer? How do you know?

- *Sales call skills.* What was said to open and close the call in a mutual way? Did the close help the customer make a decision to move along the purchase path? If concerns arose, how effectively were they resolved? How was active listening demonstrated? Impactful use of visuals? Body language and other nonverbals?

Account Coaching

Before we go into the details of account coaching, let's be clear: Account coaching is not another word for coaching opportunities in an account. Account coaching is focused on selling models where salespeople are selling into named or strategic accounts where they may manage multiple opportunities in multiple buying centers or fields of play.

Account coaching conversations focus on the broader nature of the account, the customer's strategic business context (including their customers and their marketplace), the potential the sales organization has to impact that business and the myriad of relationships that need to be initiated and nurtured through providing perspective and insights. These kinds of accounts are usually those where you are aiming for Trusted Partner status (or as close as is reasonable in your industry) as highlighted in the SRP Matrix.

Sales enablement can support these kinds of conversations through deploying account management methodologies, creating coaching diagnostic questions and guidelines for analyzing account plans, identifying technologies to uncover account information and providing tools and a visual structure for relationship mapping.

Recommended Focus for Account Coaching

- *Research and analysis.* How well have we synthesized internal and external data into a picture of the account? How

have we broken the account down into manageable segments or fields of play?

- *Focus segments*. For the segments or business units we
  are prioritizing, what are the trends they are facing? The
  opportunities they are pursuing? What are our strengths in
  being able to offer them exceptional value? What is our
  most significant vulnerability?
- *Relationship mapping*. Who are the strategic players? What
  is their authority and influence? Have we identified a
  sponsor? Coach? Others? How well have we connected
  those players to relationships by aligning them with internal resources? What's the quality of each relationship?
  What are the relationship gaps that need to be closed as
  soon as possible? How do these players perceive our organization? How is this perception different regarding certain opportunities within this account?
- *Moving forward*. What focused investments may make
  sense and why? What existing investments should we stop
  based on lack of mutual value? What actions should we
  take? Marketing and sales programs to launch? What specific opportunities should be added to the pipeline?

Territory Coaching

Territory coaching leverages market and territory analyses, data
and definitions (usually supplied by sales operations) to keep
salespeople focused. Without this focus, salespeople can be working constantly but never get any closer to their targets. As
with account coaching, territory coaching is not about coaching opportunities in the territory. It takes a more strategic look at
how to approach the territory: the right accounts, industries and
buyer roles.

Sales enablement supports this coaching by deploying territory management tools and working with sales operations to create manager level dashboards.

Recommended Focus for Territory Coaching

- *Target segment analysis.* What industries, verticals, customer segments are being targeted within the territory? Why? What data is being used to validate, narrow down or expand the focus areas?
- *Focused buyer role.* What is the most important buyer role for certain products and services in the targeted industries and customer segments? What's the (social) engagement strategy? What are the specific value messages that attract this buyer role?
- *Action planning.* What is being done to increase presence within the key segments identified? What networks are being leveraged? How to evaluate progress?

How to Coach Is as Critical as What to Coach

In order to help managers facilitate these varied conversations, your coaching enablement services should cover: processes, skills and tools.

> *Coaching Processes.* Coaches should conduct a kickoff where they set expectations for how the process will work, the topics that will be discussed and the tools that will be used. This should be followed by a regular cadence of formal, scheduled coaching sessions. Coaching ideally happens in the moment, of course. But that is not a substitute for formal coaching sessions, in person or virtual. Especially in the beginning when organizations implement sales coaching, scheduling formal coaching sessions is important. The better the implementation progresses, the easier it will become for sales managers to leverage every coaching moment. Pay particular attention to coaching on a sales call. Coaching calls are distinct from joint calls where both coaches and salespeople are in selling roles.

Coaching Skills. Coaching conversations should mirror sales conversations, focusing on providing perspective and insights, asking lots of questions and allowing the salespeople to come to conclusions on next steps, agree on diagnoses, etc. Focus on communication skills for recognition, constructive feedback and development. While sales managers may have gone through general leadership courses, offered (or required) by Human Resources, it will be important for them to understand how such skills and processes are deployed in a sales context.

Coaching Tools. The simplest coaching tool would be a small guideline that includes a set of sample questions for each phase of the customer's path along with covering different selling scenarios. More sophisticated coaching tools are those that are integrated with your CRM system, providing related data, analytics and additional insights from call recordings and other customer interactions.

Avoid Common Pitfalls

Successfully deploying coaching services isn't easy. If it were, we would see a lot more organizations with dynamic coaching maturity. Let's discuss a few hurdles that we see consistently derail coaching services.

Confusing managing activities with coaching behaviors. Another nuance of coaching that sometimes gets lost in practice is the difference between activities and behaviors. Activities are what the salesperson does, and these activities can often be counted. For example, if you know that it takes an average of three interactions with an interested prospect before they convert to an opportunity, you might encourage the salesperson to not give up after one. That may be helpful, but it's not coaching. It's activity management.

Sales coaching focuses on what the salesperson says and does during those calls. How well is the salesperson

using every opportunity to interact with a prospect or customer to provide relevant, valuable perspectives?

Viewing coaching as exclusively manager to salesperson. By definition, most sales managers have experience and come to
their role with a firmly ingrained idea of what it means
to coach, which they learned from the coaches (good and
bad) in their careers. If the sales manager has been in the
role for any length of time, these approaches will have
become even more entrenched. Training, and probably
lots of it, will be required to replace old behaviors with
new ones. This training will need to be supplemented with
reinforcement activities and coaching from the sales manager's managers. Their leaders will need to model what
good coaching looks like. In addition, many organizations
find peer-to-peer coaching effective. It helps if other sales
managers have someone they can emulate, especially if
that individual is turning in better than average results.

Not ensuring that coaches have the right domain expertise. For
sales managers, expertise is required in various areas, such
as having selling expertise, industry expertise, business
acumen, and, of course, expertise in all areas salespeople
are equipped with by sales enablement. In whatever area
they coach, they have to know what they are coaching on.
Especially when it comes to methodologies, processes and
specific skills such as value messaging, sales managers have
to be more than familiar with the topic. Sales managers are
tasked with so much that, for instance, many times they
are given shorter versions of methodology training. This
comes back to haunt you in coaching. Those in coaching roles must be domain experts in the methodologies
that they are going to coach and reinforce. They need
whatever services you offer the sales team and should
receive extra services to help them align their coaching
(for example, a manager version of a sales process course
that teaches how to coach salespeople at each step of that
process).

Overinvesting time in administration and skimping on coaching.
Time, and the lack thereof, is the proverbial elephant
in the room. We ask a lot, sometimes too much, of our
sales managers (forecasting, completing reports, attending
meetings), and they are legitimately overwhelmed. As a
result, coaching takes a back seat. The *CSO Insights 2017*
Sales Enablement Optimization Study shows that sales managers have an average of 6 to 10 direct reports and spend
less than 30 minutes per week per salesperson coaching in
any given area.

Let's put that in context with an example that is pretty typical based on our experience and that of the thousands of organizations we've worked with. If a sales manager has eight direct
reports and spends one hour a week coaching each salesperson on opportunities and skills plus a half hour a month with
each of them on funnel coaching and another hour a month on
account/territory coaching, that's 8 to 11 hours a week spent on
coaching—roughly a quarter of the manager's time.

Part of the answer is to simply make coaching a priority. Invest
in it, resource it, hold people accountable for it. Even so, time
remains scarce. The good news is that new artificial intelligence
driven tools are available to capture data (right down to the
words sellers use in a sales call), diagnose coaching issues and
make recommendations on actions that will drive better results,
all served up to coaches and salespeople in intuitive dashboards
and reports.

Miller Heiman Group, for example, has built software for real-
time coaching aligned to the Strategic Selling® sales methodology. Such tools use analytics to pinpoint which opportunities are highest priority, what actions will advance an opportunity and which team members should be a coaching priority based on pipeline health and key deals. This means coaches
can invest the time they would have spent digging up information into more fruitful coaching discussions and salesperson
development.

AI Enables Real-time Analysis of Sales Calls

Artificial intelligence (AI) is now poised to not only help sales-people get more meetings, but also help them more effectively conduct those meetings. One example of this is a solution from San Francisco-based Chorus.ai. Its platform automatically captures and analyzes sales calls in real time. One company leveraging this platform is AdRoll, which has been recognized by *Inc.* magazine as the fastest-growing advertising company two years in a row.

Sam Trachtenberg is vice president of operations for AdRoll. In talking to Sam about his company's experiences with AI, he noted that since fully implementing the system in January 2017, keyword searchable audio and text files are created for each sales meeting. Salespeople and sales management can then easily review them.

"What we are really getting a lot of benefit out of is that with Chorus we are able to surface the best calls," Sam said, "and we have created our own greatest hits playlist. We are making legends out of our salespeople by featuring the top 20 calls where our people went in and really killed it during a customer meeting. That is especially useful to new salespeople to learn what *great* looks like."

Based on usage, Chorus is providing AdRoll with active KPIs, such as total number of calls per salesperson and number of minutes per call. But it doesn't stop there. Sam shared that, "The system can assess how often our salespeople are using *filler* words versus *value* words. It can also tell you the number of calls where the value prop was *not* delivered." Based on these metrics, AdRoll can easily tie call performance back to sales performance in terms of close rates, average deal size, etc.

When asked what his biggest surprises were in moving to AI-based sales enablement, Sam shared that, "I expected there to be some level of resistance from salespeople thinking this was too much like big brother watching them or customers balking at having the calls recorded. But that didn't happen. I was also surprised by how high the adoption was on the part of sales managers. They are very interested in knowing what their people are doing, and they get a lot out of putting on their headsets and listening to key aspects of a sales call."

Evolving Your Coaching Maturity

The approach for organizing your coaching services is much like what we outlined in the chapters on content and training. However, there's a good chance that this area will need more effort than others, given that these services may not currently exist. Here are four key steps to take.

1. *Take stock of where you are and what you have.* Start by understanding the maturity of sales coaching in your organization today. As described at the onset of this chapter:
   - *Random*: Coaching (how/when/whether to do it) left up to the sales manager.
   - *Informal*: Some guidance on how to coach but no reinforcement or accountability.
   - *Formal*: Prescribed process with training and accountability for use.
   - *Dynamic*: Extends formal approach by alignment with an enablement framework.

   As you can see in Figure 7.4, there was positive movement from 2016 to 2017. However, most organizations still have a long way to go to master sales coaching. You will want to consider your starting point as you think through what services you should prioritize.

   Then, create an inventory of all your coaching services, including supporting content and training. If coaching hasn't been emphasized in the past, there probably won't be much, but a search for unofficial services might yield results. For example, sales managers who are good at coaching (whether they learned from a former manager or

Figure 7.4 Organizations' Coaching Approach

developed the skills on their own) often create tools for use during their coaching conversations. You might even consider listing these experienced coaches as an asset in themselves for peer-to-peer coaching.

You might also find general coaching training being offered as an element of existing leadership courses. These existing services can be used to build the foundation for your coaching services.

When inventorying services, remember to include any data or analyses your sales managers have to work with and the delivery mechanisms in place for serving the information up to them in a relevant way. Often, there is far more data available than is being used. It either just takes too long to find it or coaches don't know how to use it.

2. *Gather feedback and data.* As always, gather anecdotal feedback from your audience to determine what they find valuable and what they think they need. If they've never experienced what it means to have a good coach, especially in a sales context, they may not have given it much thought, but the way they see and express their challenges can tell you quite a bit about what they need. Plus, they usually appreciate being asked.

You will also want to talk with salespeople to see how well they think their managers are coaching them. You'll probably get a wide variety of answers, depending on what the sales professionals think it means to "coach." A better way of phrasing the questions might be, "In what ways does your manager help you reach your full potential?" and "How could your manager do better?"

There may also be exit interview data to mine from discussions with departed salespeople.

As for data, remember to include sales operations in your research as they are usually responsible for defining the selling process to which your coaching services must be aligned. They can provide feedback on how well the prescribed methodologies are being followed. This will give you an indication of the areas in which your coaches need more development. For example, if forecasts are always wildly inaccurate, sales managers may need guidance on how to coach salespeople to identify the opportunities most likely to close. This is a good example of how coaches can connect the internal selling processes to the customer's path.

Data might also include analyzing which sales managers consistently reach their targets. These managers may or may not be thought of as "natural coaches," but understanding the approaches and tools they use when interacting with salespeople can give you an indication of what works.

3. *Assess your assets.* Now, go through your list of assets and decide what's useful and what isn't, based on the gaps uncovered in your data collection and your goals as stated in your charter. For example, if the data that sales managers need to coach effectively exists, but they aren't using it, are services needed to teach them how the data correlates to performance? Or, if the data isn't easily accessible, would new delivery mechanisms, such as role-specific dashboards, help?

4. *Prioritize and act on gaps.* If your enablement discipline is relatively new, you'll probably have plenty of gaps. As with content and training, you may have gaps along the customer's

path. For example, there may be plenty of guidelines that help sales managers coach an opportunity in the awareness phase, but no guidelines that help the sales manager develop the sales professional's ability to communicate value delivered in the implementation and adoption phase.

You might also have gaps in one or more of the five coaching areas we talked about at the beginning of this chapter. As we stated earlier, opportunity coaching is where sales managers tend to spend the most time. They may need additional services to help them develop their skills when it comes to funnel, account and territory coaching.

Of course, when assessing gaps, you should also take the feedback you gathered into account. Not every coaching service neatly corresponds to either the coaching area or the customer's path. Listening to what sales managers say they need is the key to success.

If It Were Only that Easy—Coaching Is Just the Beginning

We'd be remiss if we didn't point out that coaching is just one piece of broader sales manager enablement. Sales managers are enablement audience, too, and not just as recipients of coaching training.

Being in a sales manager role is the hardest and most complex job in sales. Think of sales management as the mastery of three areas that must be managed simultaneously: customers, business and people (see Figure 7.5).

Customers. Ensuring that the go-to-market strategy is executed with customers as well as working directly with customers in the sales process.

People. Recruiting, onboarding and developing salespeople and sales teams into full productivity, leveraging their full potential.

Business. Functioning as the liaison between the business and the frontline salespeople including forecasting, reporting, analysis and more.

Figure 7.5 The Sales Manager Triangle

This is a tall order, and yet most sales managers will tell you that they have received little training or tools, learning their job as they go along to varying degrees of success. This is validated by the *2017 CSO Insights Sales Enablement Optimization Study*, which found that 14% of organizations did not make any training investments in their sales managers at all, and 42% were spending $1,500 or less per person.

Yet, those that did make the investment outperformed those that did not in terms of quota attainment, win rates and revenue plan attainment. So, yes, start with coaching services to support frontline sales success. Be aware that coaching is the most impactful skill to be developed in sales managers but not the only skill to care about. In the triangle shown in Figure 7.5, coaching sits in the people area. As it is a new skill, the effort shouldn't be underestimated. But as you advance your sales enablement function, grow it to build out a full-fledged strategy for sales manager enablement that covers all areas of the sales manager triangle. And that means you need to enrich their knowledge and expertise in the customer and the business area, just think about, for example, domain expertise, business acumen, data analysis, team leadership, forecasting/business processes, hiring and more.

Up Next

So far, we've shown how content, training and coaching services all work to enable the entire sales force. It's likely that these services will be created and deployed via a range of resources and departments. Therefore, it will be important to ensure that they are aligned and integrated with each other.

In our final chapter on enablement services, we'll discuss value messaging and its role in sales force enablement as the glue that ensures that customer-facing content, internal enablement content, training and coaching services are consistent and effective.

Questions to Consider

- What maturity level is coaching at within our organization?
- How effective are our coaches at each type of coaching? What training and content exists to assist managers (and others) with each kind of coaching?
- How much time do our managers spend on sales coaching?
- What level of resource is devoted to sales manager enablement?

Immediate Actions

Jot down two or three immediate actions you should take to improve the coaching services you provide.

8

Creating Consistency Through Value Messaging

Key Points

- Value messaging is the glue that aligns enablement services and creates the consistency salespeople need to be effective.
- Salespeople need value messages all along the customer's path, but the types of value messaging differ by phase.
- Ideally, enablement does not create value messaging, but it may need to take more of a leadership role in orchestrating it if the organization's current efforts are insufficient or value messaging is not well understood.

Value Messaging Is the Glue That Aligns Enablement Services

Alignment to the customer's path is an external way of looking at alignment, but we also need to look at alignment between services because it creates the consistency salespeople need to be effective and reinforces your investments in enablement. It also reduces confusion and adds to your credibility when services are clearly created in tandem and designed to work together.

Consider this all-too-common scenario: The product marketing team has created messaging for a new product launch. This messaging goes into the team's online content, its demand generation campaigns and all the customer-facing materials the team produces. Product management creates product training for the launch, but its training and related content is crafted from a product perspective that is aligned neither to the customer's path nor to the messaging created by marketing. Enablement has already provided a playbook for the product line, but the new launch makes much of the messaging in it obsolete.

Imagine what this lack of consistency means for the sales force. Here are the kinds of complaints we hear from salespeople every day. "Product training only covered the features and functions of the new product." "Marketing messaging isn't sales-ready, and it doesn't work." "The new messaging doesn't match our playbooks or the training we just went through. Nothing fits together."

What is your sales force likely to do? They will simply switch off the noise and ignore everything. They won't use any of the new assets, reverting instead to anything they already have on their laptops, such as enablement's outdated playbook. That's probably not what and how you want them to sell.

Value messaging provides the necessary input to those creating internal and customer-facing content. Value messages are the central themes that run through all these services, providing consistency for both salespeople and relevant buyers. Additionally, if you are working with various relevant buyer roles, you have a role-based value messaging approach to address each role appropriately. Effective value messaging deserves a dynamic approach that follows the same design point: the customer's path. These kinds of scenarios can be resolved when value messaging is created for every phase of the customer's path, then used consistently

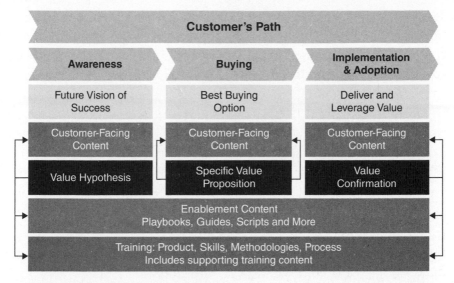

Figure 8.1 Value Messaging's Role in the Sales Enablement Framework

in customer-facing materials and throughout all of the new and updated enablement services.

We've added arrows to the enablement services framework to show the alignment between services, but the key addition to the framework is the value messaging layer between customer-facing content and enablement content (see Figure 8.1). Alignment happens when this layer is complete and consistent value messages flow upward into customer-facing content and downward into enablement content.

This may seem like an obvious concept, but data from the *CSO Insights 2017 Sales Enablement Optimization Study* shows just how uncommon it is. Only 35% of respondents said their services were aligned at the value messaging level.

What Is Value Messaging?

Before we get into enablement's role in value messaging, let's talk for a moment about the different types of value messages. At a high level, value messages describe how a product, service or a solution helps the customer solve a challenge and achieve their desired objectives and outcomes. However, because value messages need to be aligned to the customer's path, the type of value message used varies at each phase. There is no such thing as a one-size-fits-all value proposition.

In the awareness phase, *value hypotheses* address the customer's current challenges and help the customer envision a better future state. Without this vision buyers have no reason to change their current state and enter the buying phase so the deal stalls.

In the awareness phase, *value hypotheses* address the customer's current challenges and help the customer envision a better future state. Without this vision, buyers have no reason to change their current state and enter the buying phase so the deal stalls. In a world where self-informed customers often come to the table with preconceived notions about a solution, these messages also help salespeople add perspectives that inspire buyers to think differently about their challenges and opportunities and change their concept of how best to approach them.

Ultimately, salespeople have to develop a future vision of success with their prospects and customers to convert a lead into an opportunity. Value hypotheses are used to create content such as case studies and success stories as they show how other customers addressed similar situations successfully, ideally with measurable results. Role-based, high-level presentations that focus on a business problem, its impact on the business and how to approach a resolution and achieve the desired results are also created with this type of value message.

In the buying phase, *specific value propositions* help the buyer choose the best buying option.

In the buying phase, *specific value propositions* help the buyer choose the best buying option by focusing on the values and benefits of the proposed solution and mapping it to the customer's desired results and wins. At this phase, sales professionals must prove that their solution is the option that best helps all the members of the buying team achieve their desired results and wins and their shared future vision of success. At this stage, specific value propositions are often related to products and services, but always and only in the context of the customer's business challenges, its buying team's different viewpoints, and its desired results and wins.

> In the implementation and adoption phase, *value confirmation messages* build a foundation for future business.

Value confirmation messages are the foundation for developing long-lasting customer relationships and growth within existing accounts. Projects are often delegated to new stakeholders during implementation and adoption. So, on the one hand, it is essential that sales professionals build and develop relationships with these new individuals. On the other hand, they should never forget to communicate the value that has been created to the initial sponsors of the project. Paying attention to value confirmation messages helps sales professionals identify additional opportunities to create additional value for these customers. These messages are often overlooked, but they are essential to ensuring additional business with a newly created customer or further developing business within an already existing account.

To be clear, value messages are not about pushing products. They are about helping the sales professional connect to the customers' business challenges, their expected results and wins and their specific context. In the latter phase of the customer's path, especially in the buying phase, they may contain more product-specific statements, but they are still about what the solution means to the customer.

Furthermore, value messaging must be adapted to the customer's context for a given buying decision. That's why the playbooks we discussed in the content chapter are so valuable. By creating playbooks for different scenarios, such as industry or buyer role, enablement can help salespeople adapt the appropriate message to the customer's path, their business context and their individual and group wins.

Orchestrating the Process

Enablement rarely creates messaging. (Ideally never.) More typically, value messages come from a collaboration between marketing or product marketing and product management. However, the same challenges we discussed when we talked about marketing-created content happen with marketing-created messaging. Because marketing is primarily focused on demand and lead generation and the early awareness phase, latter phases of the customer's path are overlooked.

By allying with marketing, sales force enablement can assure messages are available and aligned all along the customer's path. In organizations where value messaging and how it changes along the customer's path is not well understood, enablement might need to create the structure for the individual messaging modules, develop a process for creating the messaging, and then work closely with product marketing and product management to establish the process and be sure the deliverables are completed. As your discipline evolves, value messaging will be better understood by all contributors and creating these modules should become a natural part of their roles.

Your process for creating value messages will depend heavily on how sophisticated your organization currently is at value messaging. If your marketing team has an established process in place, chances are you can piggyback on their processes, ensuring that they are expanded to cover the entire customer's path and the sales team's enablement requirements. If your organization is less sophisticated, you may need to take more of a leadership role in establishing the value messaging process and then orchestrating the entire effort.

We've put together a chart outlining the process of creating value messaging at a high level. You can use Table 8.1 to ensure that all of the steps are covered, whether you're simply expanding current efforts or establishing a value messaging project from scratch.

Once value messages are created, sales enablement plays a vital role in ensuring they are used consistently across all enablement services. (This accomplishment can earn you a great deal of points with the marketing team, as inconsistent value messaging and low adoption rates are battles they fight every day!)

Value Messaging's Impact on Performance

Some organizations are great at creating value messages. Others see it as a waste of time and don't allocate the funds and resources needed to do a proper job. They'd prefer enablement and other functions spend their time creating the materials that "sales will actually use" when engaging the buyer.

Our research shows that this is a mistake. At least 2 of the 12 World-Class sales practices that surfaced in our *2017 World Class Sales Practices Study* are directly related to value messaging:

1. We (our salespeople) are effective at *selling value* to avoid discounting or gaining comparative value in return for price concessions.
2. Our salespeople consistently and effectively communicate appropriate *value messages that are aligned* to our customers' and prospects' needs.

The 7% of respondents identified as World-Class consistently outperformed all respondents across several key metrics: revenue plan attainment, quota attainment, win-rate of forecast deals and voluntary/involuntary turnover.

Table 8.1   The Value Messaging Process

Phase 1: Assess

Assess current messaging across all customer-facing and enablement assets for:
- Effectiveness
- Consistency
- Currency
- Coverage of the customer's path

Analyze the results.

Define the next steps, such as:
- Revisiting go-to-market and go-to-customer strategies.
- Developing a value messaging framework to ensure adequate coverage of all phases.
- Create plan for addressing gaps in coverage for roles, industries, business scenarios, etc.

Phase 2: Build

Estimate the effort required and build the business case for value messaging.

Build a value messaging framework, or adjust one that is currently available.

Build a work plan for value messaging projects. Include details such as:
- Collaboration required, including any third parties.
- Road map for milestones and deliverables.
- Pilot projects, e.g., new product or service, specific industry, specific role, etc.
- Establish executive buy-in, gain the support of collaborators and allocate resources.

Table 8.1 (*continued*)

Phase 3: Create

Conduct a workshop with contributors (including third parties) for the first pilot. (Break larger messaging projects down into phases.)
- Agree on the business problem your product or service solves.
- Agree on the business value.
- Create the value messages for the most important buyer role for each phase of the customer's path.

Capture the results of the workshop in your messaging framework.

Move on to second phase of the pilot project or pilot project No. 2.

Phase 4: Integrate

Integrate value messages into enablement services:
- Update customer-facing content services.
- Update internal enablement services such as playbooks, selling scripts, tools, etc.
- Update or integrate new value messages in related product training services.
- Create new services as needed, such as micro-learning modules focused on a key buyer role.
- Update or integrate coaching training services, coaching processes as necessary and coaching guidelines.
- Collaborate with marketing on updates of customer-facing content such as websites and brochures.

Phase 5: Implement

Implement the new value messaging approach:
- Create a curriculum for all relevant customer-facing roles.
- Ensure attendance for related product/value messaging training services.
- Ensure SECM platform is updated with current content services.
- Conduct special coaching sessions with sales managers to ensure they are ready to reinforce value messaging.
- Gather feedback from all involved roles.
  - Refine messaging.
  - Adjust processes.

Next Up

We've completed our survey of enablement services and the value messaging needed to align services and connect them to the customer's path. You should have a pretty good idea of what you need to create, adjust or remove. Now the question is: How will you get it all done with the resources you have? That will be the focus of Part Four.

Questions to Consider

- How well are our services aligned to each other?
- What challenges has our lack of alignment caused? For example, is sales ignoring some or all of our enablement efforts or have we not seen the anticipated results?
- What value messaging is already being created by either enablement or other functions like marketing?
- Do these messaging modules cover the entire customer's path?
- What other gaps do we have in key areas such as industry, business challenge or buyer role?

Immediate Actions

Jot down two to three actions you should take to better align your enablement services.

PART

IV

The Inner Workings
of Enablement

IN PART FOUR, we'll turn to the inner workings of enablement, starting with that most important of concepts: collaboration. The unavoidable truth is you won't get it all done if you try to do it all yourself. If we haven't said it enough, enablement is a collaborative effort and your primary role is to orchestrate the efforts of others to create consistent and effective enablement services all along the customer's path. Cross-functional collaboration is seldom easy, but defining a formal, repeatable approach can make the process a lot smoother and more efficient.

After collaboration, we'll take a detailed look at another vital aspect of enablement: enablement technology. You've probably already noticed that many of the case studies and examples we've provided throughout the first three sections of this book involve technology. That's because technology has become such an integral component of enablement that those organizations that don't leverage technology effectively risk putting themselves at a severe competitive disadvantage.

However, as with everything else in enablement, investing in technology requires prioritization, both because no organization has an unlimited budget for technology and because some technologies are more foundational than others. In Chapter 10, we'll provide a little more structure around the various types of enablement technology and how they can help.

Then, we'll use Chapters 11 and 12 to focus on enablement operations, the engine that drives your enablement efforts. Operations needs two chapters because it covers so many things: the enablement processes you use to orchestrate everything from the design to the delivery of services, how you engage executive sponsors and stay in touch with changes to the organization's strategies and goals, how you solve the inevitable challenges you will encounter and how you measure success.

9

Formalized Collaboration

Key Points

- Enablement professionals must be highly skilled at getting things done through other people and departments.
- Setting up a dynamic collaboration model with clear responsibilities drives enablement productivity and scalability.
- Organizations with a more formal approach to collaboration are as much as 21% better at achieving quota than organizations with no or ad hoc collaboration approaches.

Getting the Job Done

In this chapter, we're going to talk about how you can create a scalable enablement discipline through formalized collaboration (See Figure 9.1). But before we talk about collaboration in an enablement context, we need to address a concern that some of you probably still have.

In Part One, we discussed who owns enablement, and if you'll recall, we said the only way to create consistent, effective services

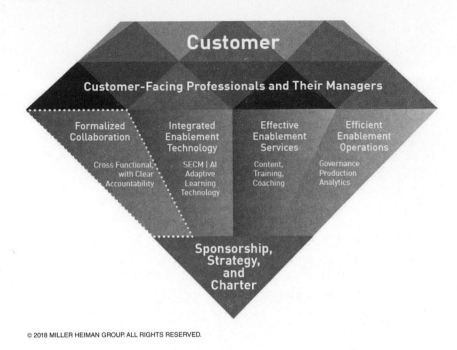

Figure 9.1 The Sales Force Enablement Clarity Model

was to make enablement a separate discipline. Then, throughout this book, we've repeatedly said that enablement doesn't (and can't) do everything. So how does that work? If enablement is a separate discipline, doesn't that mean it manages and controls the resources to produce the services that sales needs to be effective?

Not at all. Enablement professionals must be highly skilled at getting things done through other people. (And often, using someone else's budget.) There are two sides to making that happen. The first is your governance model. We laid the groundwork for that with the enablement charter, and we'll discuss it in more detail in Chapter 11 when we focus on enablement governance. The second is collaboration. Collaboration is how enablement services get created and delivered by various departments, and it is our focus for this chapter (see Figure 9.1).

What Does Effective Enablement Collaboration Look Like?

We talk a lot about collaboration in our work with sales teams. It's a fact of life for the modern workforce. But when we ask our clients what collaboration means to them in an enablement context, we get a variety of often-vague answers. For some, it just means working together and doing whatever it takes to get the job done. Others describe it in terms of visibility: "keeping others in the loop." Some even describe it as an IT tool, as though the collaboration platform sales operations is working on will solve all the challenges inherent in cross-functional collaboration.

In the context of sales force enablement, we define collaboration specifically as the process of working across functions or with third parties to provide services that help the sales force achieve better results, ideally in a shorter amount of time. Everyone agrees on the need to collaborate, but rarely do teams stop to apply any structure or formal processes to that collaboration. Instead, the focus is on short-term projects, such as producing a piece of collateral, selecting an enablement technology tool or delivering training services.

When people collaborate to complete an enablement service or to deliver on a broader enablement initiative, that's a good thing, but it's not scalable. Redefining roles and responsibilities each time a new piece of content or training needs to be delivered drags the entire organization down. There are the inevitable discussions with potential collaborators of whether the service adds any value, whether it's their job to help produce that service, and from which budget the resources should be allocated.

Setting up a formalized collaboration model can help you avoid wasting time in these sorts of negotiations and debates. But what does formalized collaboration look like? Below are some of the common attributes that will give you a good measuring stick against which to assess your collaboration maturity.

- Enablement collaboration is part of the job description for common roles such as product management, product marketing and L&D professionals.
- The process of collaboration is predictable, repeatable and proven to lead to successful outcomes.
- There is a regular cadence to meetings, both at a high level (strategic discussions with department leads, as an example) and when working on specific services.
- Meeting attendance is prioritized and individual contributors take their obligations seriously.
- Department managers ensure their people have the bandwidth to devote to enablement projects. If there are obstacles, they work to address them.
- Everyone understands the role of enablement and how it contributes to organizational performance.
- When changes happen, such as an organization strategy change or a market-impacting event, collaborators proactively consider how enablement needs to respond.

> Less than 20% of sales enablement functions have a formalized approach for collaboration across departments and organizations. Those that do see results of up to 7% better quota attainment.
>
> —*CSO Insights 2017 Sales Enablement Optimization Study*

The RACI Model

To orchestrate collaboration effectively, you must make sure everyone understands their role in the process. The RACI model (or one of its derivatives) is an approach that project managers have been using successfully for decades. This model defines participation across four roles: responsible, accountable, consulted and informed.

1. *Responsible*—These are the people who primarily do the work, even if that means delegating specific pieces to others. For

example, once a sales training service has been defined, learning and development may take the lead on pulling the project together. That makes sense because, as learning professionals, they can make essential decisions about how each component needs to function together to create the best service possible. They can also offer much-needed input and feedback to other contributors. The same is true for marketing when it comes to their specialties, such as customer-facing presentations or white papers.

2. *Accountable*—The accountable role is the individual or team whose neck is on the line, so to speak. These people may play other roles in the project as well, such as contributing a portion of the deliverable, but they get some of the credit and most of the blame for the state of the final product. In enablement, the accountable role is often the enablement team.

3. *Consulted*—These are individuals who have something to contribute to the effort, such as subject matter expertise, but they aren't responsible for any of the actual work. For example, when pulling together a messaging asset, product management might need to provide clarification on the value of a feature, but they won't be creating the value messages. Customers and industry analysts might fall into this category as well.

4. *Informed*—Finally, there are individuals who will need to be kept informed of your efforts but who won't be involved in doing any of the work. They may have feedback, but it is more likely to be high-level than specific to any activity. Your enablement advisory board, which we will talk about in Chapter 11 when we discuss enablement operations, is made up of these individuals.

> Roles should be predefined for each type of enablement service (for example, playbook, customer-facing presentation, product training) because the role an individual fills may be different for each.

These roles should be predefined for each type of enablement service (for example, playbook, customer-facing presentation, product training) because the role an individual fills may be different for each. For example, someone from sales operations might be responsible for creating a sales methodology training service, but only consulted in the production of other services. By predefining these roles by enablement service type, the cross-functional team can avoid the time spent negotiating responsibilities each time a new service is created.

"For each content type, we have defined the roles and their responsibilities and accountabilities along the enablement process. Take product launch as an example, product management knows what has to be created, and product marketing knows what has to be created and also sales enablement knows what needs to be assembled, for instance, in a playbook, or in a sales kit.

"Each role has its own charter and cadence. And we review that cadence and we obviously make changes as our business makes changes. As an example, if there is a need to reduce an outcome from 10 to 5 days, we have to discuss if and how we can make this happen.

"Part of the sales enablement team's job is to ensure that we are constantly communicating with those involved teams and helping them if there is a process change or a process update that we need. These teams are all busy, too. That's why communication is key to success."

Christine Dorrion, CallidusCloud, VP Global
Sales & Channel Operations and Enablement

Key Areas for Improvement

The *CSO Insights 2017 Sales Enablement Optimization Study* examined collaboration across 10 different functions, asking respondents to rate the level of collaboration with sales enablement in each (see Figure 9.2).

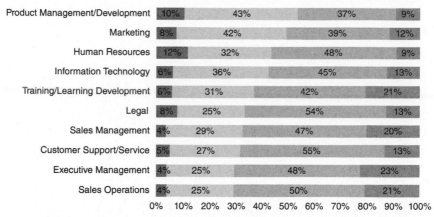

Figure 9.2 Sales Enablement Collaboration Assessment

Despite the predominantly informal nature of collaboration, it appears that it is still viewed as reasonably effective across most departments. This is a marked change from years past when few departments collaborated.

In our latest study, only two key areas remain that need improvement or major redesign: product development/ management and marketing. These are major hurdles that must be overcome. Both functions are vital to integrating content with training, coaching and other services, providing customer insights and more. Those sales enablement organizations that collaborate well with both functions report higher win rates than those that don't.

Examples of Cross-Functional Collaboration

Product Mgt./ Development	Internal product briefs, detailed customer-facing collateral and content, one-pagers, value calculation and configuration tools
Marketing	Customer-facing content in various forms, voice of customer data, campaigns, lead

	generation, lead nurturing, open market, social content
Human Resources	Hiring profiles, hiring assessment, onboarding programs, succession planning into management roles, competency modeling
Information Technology	IT integration, CRM, Sales Enablement Content Management (SECM) solutions, learning technology, sales analytics and sales intelligence tools, social selling tools, dashboard creation
Legal	Contract templates, legal attachments, SLA documents, SOW templates
Sales Management	Coaching and reinforcement support, customer and seller feedback
Customer Support/Service	Voice of customer data, content that helps customers implement and leverage products and services
Executive Management	Sponsorship, resources, access to business planning, enablement charter, governance model
Sales Operations	CRM usage, proposal templates, sales process refinements, metrics, deal approval templates, deal board templates

Selling Collaboration to the Organization

Selling collaboration to your executive sponsors can be relatively easy. Not only do those organizations that collaborate well see an improvement in quota attainment, effective collaboration can also help the organization improve its return on existing investments. Enablement can get expensive, but many of these resources are already allocated. For example, content is already being created and training services are already being offered. Enablement creates a consistency between those existing services that increases their impact on the business.

Selling collaboration to those who are expected to contribute their time and talent can be a little more difficult, especially when they see enablement as encroaching on their territory. In today's competitive business environments, there is often as much competition within the organization as there is in the market.

As we emphasized in this chapter, enablement professionals must be skilled at getting things done through other people. They must also be skilled at giving credit where credit is due. One of your roles as the leader and orchestrator of enablement services is to highlight the good work and outstanding efforts of others. Fail to do that, and you may find yourself steering a ship without a crew.

In the end, your executive sponsors charged you with the task of ensuring your cross-functional enablement discipline is working in a highly efficient mode to ensure the best outcomes possible. At the highest levels of your organization, leadership doesn't necessarily care who does what, only that it works. You'll still get to take credit where and when it counts—for the overarching productivity and performance improvements—each time you meet with your executive sponsors.

In Chapter 11, we'll expand on that by discussing the concept of the enablement advisory board and the details of the enablement production process. But first, in Chapter 10, we want to lay the groundwork for that discussion with one more vital area that needs to be covered: enablement technology.

Questions to Consider

- Have we given our enablement professionals the support they need to effectively orchestrate collaboration across all functions?
- How formal are our enablement collaboration processes?

- How effectively do we define roles, responsibilities and processes?
- With which teams do we collaborate best? Which areas are our weakest?
- What are the obstacles to collaboration in each functional area, and how can they be overcome?

Immediate Actions

Jot down two or three actions you could take to improve cross-functional collaboration in your organization.

10

Integrated Enablement Technology

Key Points

- Enablement is not typically responsible for CRM, but an effective CRM system with a high rate of adoption is a prerequisite for effective enablement.
- Enablement technology covers sales enablement content management, learning management and coaching technologies plus productivity solutions and a host of other point solutions designed to address specific needs.
- When defining an enablement technology strategy, enablement needs to consider not just the technologies it owns (such as SECM) but also other solutions that contribute to enablement (such as sales analytics). This will require close collaboration with other teams, including sales operations and IT.

Enablement Starts with CRM

The internet isn't the only technological advancement that has dramatically changed the face of selling in the past 20 years. CRM

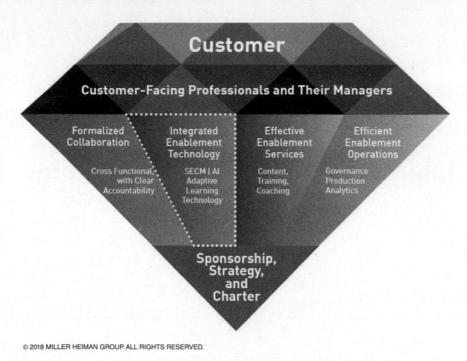

Figure 10.1 The Sales Force Enablement Clarity Model

has gone from being a system that only the most technically literate organizations and salespeople use to being the system of record for most sales organizations regardless of industry or culture (see Figure 10.1).

While most of this chapter will focus on enablement technologies, a scalable, adaptable CRM system that is widely adopted by the organization is a must-have. These systems are the anchor not only for other enablement technologies but also for the entire sales system. They are a scalable platform for productivity and performance. They provide the data necessary for insight and analysis and a single interface for the sales team. In the future, these systems will be the prerequisite for advancements such as selling augmented by AI. Organizations that are still struggling with CRM adoption and data accuracy need to address these issues or risk being left behind by their peers.

> Organizations that are still struggling with CRM adoption and data accuracy need to address these issues or risk being left behind by their peers.

Shoring Up a Shaky Foundation

Unfortunately, many CRM implementations are a rather shaky foundation for enablement. It's taken decades for CRM implementation and adoption rates to reach current levels, and adoption rates still aren't universally above the 75% level that they need to be to see real results. Furthermore, only 25% of respondents to our *2017 World-Class Sales Practices Study* say they are confident in the data in their CRM system, and only 25% agree that it improves their sales productivity.

Failed implementations and low CRM adoption rates diminish enablement's ability to measure the results of its efforts. If the data in the CRM system isn't accurate, enablement can't know whether it's helping sales be more productive or effective. This is especially true for a sales force enablement discipline that is still maturing, where the emphasis should be on leading indicators of future sales performance. This is a topic we will be discussing in more detail in Chapter 12 when we focus on enablement metrics.

While CRM implementation and adoption is usually the purview of another team (most often sales operations), enablement can help solve the problem in a couple of ways. First, if the enablement technology is designed to be used directly by the salesperson, enablement can work with IT to ensure it is integrated to CRM so that the data collected gets into the system. Second, enablement can leverage CRM to deliver services that support the methodology. For example, when sales enters an opportunity into the system, playbooks can be automatically generated based on the opportunity details. When CRM becomes the one-stop-shop for content, ideally based on an integrated sales enablement content solution, sales is more likely to turn to the CRM system for what it needs and adoption improves.

"It is important to put into context the extent to which CRM plays a pivotal role in our enablement strategy. One of our four priorities going back to 2015 was to get to a single CRM system across the business. We started an ambitious program in the summer of 2015 and just over 12 months later had 1,000 users across 24 countries using a single instance of SFCE [Salesforce] as our sole sales automation platform. This has supported our ambition to have a consistent and uniform sales process and reporting of all key sales metrics.

"This is pivotal since our strategy is to make SFCE the place where we "live" as a sales organization. As such, any enabling technologies aimed at driving effectiveness and efficiency needs to tie in to SFCE and become part of its ecosystem. A great example is how we've embedded the blue sheet [opportunity management process] via a plug-in to SFCE."

Boris Kluck, VP Sales Operations,
Cable & Wireless Communications

Enablement Technologies

Before we talk about specific enablement technologies, we should point out that there are lots of sales technologies that enablement probably won't get deeply involved in. For example, IT may be tasked with determining whether a BYOD (bring your own device) policy makes sense or whether the entire sales team needs to be equipped with company-owned (and managed) mobile technologies. Sales enablement needs to be informed of these decisions as the services it provides will need to be accessible from whatever mobile devices the team uses, but enablement probably won't be a contributor to the decision or own any part of the implementation or adoption of the solution.

That's good because enablement has enough to do staying on top of all of the possible enablement technologies available. New applications are released almost daily—so many we couldn't possibly name them all. For the purposes of our discussions, we will simply focus on the three main categories linked to services plus productivity solutions. Though, in reality, many of the examples we provide cross categories, and sometimes, even defy categorization. Nevertheless, thinking about them in terms of categories can help enablement make sure it has its bases covered.

Sales Enablement Content Management

Today, a new evolution of content management systems called Sales Enablement Content Management (SECM) allow the salesperson to directly interact with the system, ideally through a single interface, to search for content assets based on specific criteria such as the buyer's current stage on the customer's path, the involved buyer roles, the buyer's industry and business challenges. This advanced functionality substantially reduces the time it takes for a sales professional to locate the right asset for a buyer at a particular point in the customer's path as well as all the internally needed content such as guidelines, scripts or playbooks.

More advanced SECM systems integrate with CRM to not only allow the salesperson to search for content, but also to proactively suggest content to the sales professional based on the customer's business challenges and the specific selling scenario. Some systems can automatically create playbooks and other content assets based on the attributes of the opportunity. Using this recommended content, the sales professional can adapt their approach and customize presentations.

Online Playbooks Help an Insurance Agency Increase Revenue per Employee by More than 22%

The employee benefits division of a bank-owned insurance agency had spent the last five years rolling out a sophisticated new sales methodology to a strong team of internal experts. Despite topline growth, the lack of processes and systems within the agency caused challenges with internal efficiency, and overall revenue per employee had been declining.

The company retained Code SixFour, a software company specializing in solutions for health insurance agencies—the name Code SixFour comes from the SIC (Standard Industrial Classification) industry code for insurance agents and brokers—to help define best practices and organize existing internal intellectual property and assets. After defining workflows, roles and responsibilities for all consulting project types, the team created playbooks that were automatically generated using the Code SixFour Benefits Consulting Cloud—a web-based content management solution for insurance agents and brokers. These playbooks include content such as:

- Product/solution positioning statements.
- Benchmarking data to diagnose client issues.
- Implementation tools and project plans.
- Sales discovery questions and guides.

Increasing the formality of the consulting approach and making the playbook materials accessible online vastly improved the ROI on the existing sales training investment. The tightly integrated team of producers and account managers were able to take on more ambitious projects and increase overall agency revenues by more than 22% per employee.

These integrated solutions are also much better equipped to help sales force enablement professionals, content marketers and others track how prospects and buyers use content and what the impact is. As an example, they can answer detailed questions such as: Does sharing this case study lead more often to a follow-up interaction as compared to sharing another one? Do customers read this white paper in its entirety or only view certain pages? What percentage of customers who are sent an interactive ROI tool use it, and how often does that lead to a next step, an additional question, another meeting or directly to a proposal? The same kind of analytics can be leveraged for internal enablement content to learn how, for instance, a certain playbook is used, a guideline is downloaded or a battle card is viewed.

SECM systems also offer content management functionality that can help you determine when it is time to refresh or replace content. When a specific piece of content is no longer used or no longer helping sales professionals move customers forward on their path, that's a good sign that the asset has outlived its usefulness. Replacing or refreshing old content, such as a case study that has become dated, improves sales productivity because sales professionals can more easily find what they need. It also gives them a higher level of confidence in the quality of the materials in the system.

Examples of SECM systems include: Bigtincan, Brainshark, CallidusCloud, HighSpot, MobilPaks, Savo, Seismic, Showpad and many others.

Learning Platforms

Learning platforms, including but not limited to learning management systems (LMS), are often not considered to be enablement systems, especially when they are owned and managed by L&D, but they are an important component of an integrated enablement discipline.

Traditional LMS started out as a way for teams, such as L&D and HR, to offer online learning modules and to track participation in offline and classroom training performance on any required quizzes or exams. In fact, Treion Muller, noted online learning expert, says that many learning platforms are still owned and managed by the HR department. This is another area that calls for orchestrated collaboration led by sales force enablement. If learning platforms are to become part of the sales force enablement infrastructure, the enablement team must convince executives of the benefits of an expanded view of learning systems in order to change the status quo.

As organizations discover the enablement benefits of offering bite-sized, online learning modules, training services (especially those that focus on knowledge transfer or serve as a reminder on how to use a specific message or apply a particular methodology) are being treated more and more like content assets. Ideally, these assets should be made accessible through the CRM system to provide the sales professional learning modules related to specific opportunities in a variety of e-learning and mobile formats.

Examples of systems that offer learning functionality include Brainshark, CallidusCloud Litmos and Intrepid.

Coaching

Artificial intelligence and other technology advancements are making coaching systems more efficient than ever. Management has been recording sales conversations for a while, but newer functionality allows managers to search for key words, phrases and behaviors to uncover problem areas or to understand how professionals are using value messaging in their interactions with prospects and customers. (Refer to Chapter 8 for more on value messaging.) In addition, new tools like virtual reality that simulate sales calls complete with branching scenarios based on the salesperson's responses, turn role-playing into an RPG-like experience and give sales managers an even better tool for evaluating skills. These types of tools are especially valuable for coaching remote employees. We predict a tremendous leap forward in coaching systems and capabilities as AI-augmented selling tools become more commonplace.

A few examples include 5600blue, Brainshark, Gainsight, Mindtickle, Refract, SpearFysh and Xvoyant.

Improving Coaching with AI

Gainsight is a leading Customer Success Management platform that empowers companies with a scalable way to leverage technology to drive revenue and increase customer retention. Like all companies, Gainsight is looking to drive the success of its own business as well. This led Ryan Toben, vice president revenue operations, to seek out new tools to improve forecast visibility and accuracy. The answer he found was People.ai, a platform that analyzes how salespeople spend their time, providing sales managers with the insights they need to coach their sales teams to success.

But People.ai isn't just any coaching tool. It has the capability to analyze thousands of metrics. As Toben explains, "People.ai not only tells me how long it took a salesperson to get back to a customer, it also tells me how long it took a customer to get back to the salesperson. That first metric is useful as a compliance checkpoint, but the real value is in the second metric. If we can surface the specific things that salespeople are doing to motivate customers to get back to them quickly and keep the process moving, then we can provide real benefit to the sales teams by sharing those best practices."

Productivity Solutions

This category of enablement technologies covers a wide range of solutions, including functionality available from leading enablement technology providers as well as a host of point solutions designed to address specific needs.

These applications aren't always the responsibility of enablement, but as you research the needs of your sales force, you'll likely run across opportunities to add value here, whether you're leading the effort or just calling attention to the need. If you uncover a time-waster, chances are there's an app that addresses it.

Examples in this category include: Clearslide and Jive (collaboration, engagement), Concur (expense reporting), Doodle (meeting scheduler), Five9 (predictive dialing for call centers), Gainsight, Kapta, Revegy (key account management), Go-to-Meeting and Skype (meetings and events), InsideView and Sales Navigator (sales intelligence) and RO Innovation (reference requests).

"Enablement technology plays a big role at CallidusCloud. We are now using the concept of portals. That means that every single prospect and customer has their unique portal. Our salespeople use these portals to share relevant and valuable content with them, depending on the different phase of their customer journey and the specific problem they want to solve. These portals are our single source of truth. It's extremely valuable for both because prospects and customers can give our salespeople feedback and ask questions, so that they can help them with specific and tailored content to move a deal forward. As an enablement team, we also learn a lot about different buyer roles and their different requirements regarding value messaging."

Christine Dorrion, CallidusCloud, VP Global Sales & Channel Operations and Enablement

AI-augmented selling is a technology to watch as it will enhance the capabilities of every type of selling and enablement technology. As systems become better and better at analyzing data and learning from results, they will be able to guide salespeople every step of the way: the best messages to use, the best content to share and the best next steps to take. It will be like having a World-Class sales coach at their disposal 24/7.

Sales force enablement professionals have an outstanding opportunity to add value to the organization and elevate their strategic position by staying one step ahead of these technological advancements. We'll get more into AI-augmented selling and other related topics in the final chapter: The Future of Selling.

Getting the Data You Need

When enablement doesn't own a technology, but benefits from its application and adoption, it is vital for enablement to work closely with the teams that do own the technology. Enablement may not make decisions about what technology gets acquired, but it has a lot to contribute to the discussion when the technology impacts its ability to enable sales.

> Enablement may not make decisions about what technology gets acquired, but it has a lot to contribute to the discussion when the technology impacts its ability to enable sales.

We already talked about this at the beginning of this chapter when we discussed CRM as the foundation for effective enablement. Sales operations typically owns CRM, but enablement needs to stay involved and can help ensure its adoption once implemented.

Sales analytics tools are another category of technology that enablement probably won't own, but which is fundamental to enablement achieving its goals. Analytics tools provide deeper insights by analyzing data from a variety of sources, such as CRM, enterprise resource planning (ERP) and customer service, to help sales leadership better understand and optimize sales processes. This insight is vital to your sales managers' coaching efforts.

These tools also provide the metrics that enablement uses to measure success. (We'll talk more about metrics in Chapter 12.) Again, the leading CRM and enablement application providers include powerful analytical tools in their applications. But if yours isn't quite meeting your needs or you want to perform a deeper analysis to find a solution to a particular challenge, there are plenty of integrated third-party applications on the market. Collaborating with sales operations and IT can ensure you have the data you need.

"One of the things I have never been shy about is taking the risk of exploring new technologies, so we have been leveraging AI for a couple years now. Our first exposure to AI for sales was with a company called Implicit, which was subsequently acquired by Salesforce, and it became the foundational basis for Einstein as part of Sales Cloud Lightning.

"What initially attracted me to Implicit was that it represented a way for my salespeople to have all their emails intelligently logged to the right account and opportunity in Salesforce. Our team members are sending out 50-, 60-plus emails a day. So, that capability alone generated a time savings of five or six hours a week for each of our salespeople by avoiding having to tag emails manually. We also saw an increase in data quality, as AI was able to execute this process in a way that ensured everything was done consistently and correctly."

Kai Yu Hsiung, Chief Growth Officer, Silverline

Making the Case for Enablement Technologies

Sales leaders understand the role productivity and efficiency play in achieving their goals. Here are some of the top improvements seen from sales enablement technology investments in our *CSO Insights 2017 Sales Enablement Optimization Study*:

1. Salesperson access to sales content and tools.
2. Reducing search time for content and collateral.
3. Increasing win rates.
4. Improving sales and marketing alignment.
5. Reducing new salesperson ramp-up time.

These findings can strengthen your business case for new technology investments. However, to be most effective, enablement technology must be seen as a component of a holistic enablement discipline, and your case should be made in light of your enablement charter. What organizational goals did you uncover during your discovery phase? How can you tie enablement technologies back to those goals?

Finally, another benefit of sales enablement technology that should not be discounted is that it increases the productivity of the enablement team. SECM solutions, for example, allow enablement teams to efficiently structure, organize, maintain and provide content and training services to their target audiences. Learning technologies offer enablement professionals a way to deliver effective training services in quick, easy-to-access formats. In addition, these solutions provide the analytics to determine which services approaches are most effective.

Defining Your Technology Strategy

Technology investments are big decisions. A large organization may spend a substantial portion of its budget on a single system. A good decision can translate into a real competitive advantage. A bad decision can hinder productivity and performance for years. Enablement can lead the way by creating a solid enablement technology strategy that ensures technology provides the sustainable competitive advantage leadership is looking for.

Here are three steps that can help you define your needs and gain the necessary commitment from the organization.

1. *Identify missing technologies.* Even if you're just starting to treat sales force enablement as a discipline, chances are good you have some enablement technologies already in place. However, chances are equally good that you have gaps in many of the functional areas. For example, you may have a decent SECM system and some functionality in terms of sales analytics and intelligence, a limited LMS and nothing at all for coaching. Make note of those areas where additional investments are needed and plot these on the roadmap in your charter.

    We can't stress enough how important it is to reflect the current state of enablement technology in your charter as well as to plot future needs on your roadmap. Your roadmap includes your future objectives, and at least some of these objectives will no doubt be contingent on the support of key technologies. When your organization's senior leaders approve your strategy, they need to see the entire plan to understand what future investments they will be required to make.

2. *Identify functional gaps*. Even if you have some areas covered at a high level, the functionality within the technology may not be sufficient for your needs. For example, your SECM system may be a proprietary system that cannot be integrated to your current CRM system. Or maybe it's the CRM system that is not sophisticated enough to allow integration of SECM, learning platforms and other enablement technologies. As you get your sales force enablement discipline off the ground, these technologies may serve their purpose, but at some future date, you will need to address the issue.

   Also, consider your access to the data you need to assess the impact of your efforts. If you can't get the data from your existing CRM system, you'll need to build that into your technology strategy roadmap. If your CRM system has the ability to capture the data, but usage is so low that the data can't be trusted, that's a problem that will need to be addressed. Enablement technologies that are easier to use and integrate into CRM to ensure data capture may be part of the resolution.

3. *Prioritize your investments*. If you're like most organizations, you'll be facing some daunting gaps and will need to prioritize your investments. Refer to the goals you set in your charter, especially those related to performance. Which technologies will best help you reach them?

Just as the goals in your charter are laid out on a roadmap, your technology investments should be, too. If a specific milestone or objective cannot be achieved before a functional gap is addressed, you need to record this. For example, one of your first goals might be to shorten the time sales spends looking for or creating content. To do this, you have decided to create automatically generated playbooks based on data entered into the CRM system. However, if your current SECM system doesn't have the necessary functionality or your CRM system does not allow for that kind of integration, those shortcomings will need to be addressed for you to achieve that objective.

Start Small, but Think Big

If enablement technology is lacking in your organization, resist the urge to do it all at once. As we noted earlier, technology projects can be expensive (and disruptive), so starting with a smaller project linked to a tangible benefit that is based on the overall vision can help you prove the value you add and make it easier for you to gain support and funding for future, larger projects.

If you decide to focus your efforts on a larger project, especially one that will impact a global sales force, consider starting with a pilot project. This will help minimize disruption to the sales force. Plus, those salespeople who have personally experienced the benefits can become vocal advocates for your efforts and help ensure adoption of the new technologies and related processes as you roll them out to the rest of the team.

Either way, starting with a vision in mind and working backward (based on your charter), will help you focus your investments in technology and make smarter decisions.

Questions to Consider

- How well does our current sales enablement technology support our enablement strategy and needs? What categories are we missing? What functional requirements?
- What weaknesses in our current CRM system will need to be addressed before it can serve as a stable foundation for enablement?
- Which technologies does enablement own in our organization and which technologies are owned by other

functions? How well do the teams collaborate in each of these areas of technology?

- Is our enablement technology strategy realistic and in line with our enablement maturity, or are we trying to do too much at once?

Immediate Actions

Jot down two or three actions you can take to better leverage sales technology to support sales force enablement.

11

Enablement Operations

Key Points

- Enablement operations is the backbone that ensures your enablement discipline is efficient, consistent, scalable and closely aligned to the strategies and objectives of the business.
- Enablement operations includes three primary components: governance, production and analytics.
- Your charter and collaboration model are the underlying foundation for enablement operations.

Enablement Operations Defined

Enablement operations (see Figure 11.1) is the fourth and final facet in the middle of our Sales Force Enablement Clarity Model. Like the formalized collaboration and integrated enablement technology facets, enablement operations is a structural prerequisite to creating an efficient, scalable and effective enablement discipline that can easily adapt to your changing and growing business needs.

Figure 11.1 The Sales Force Enablement Clarity Model

Enablement operations builds on the solid foundation provided by a well-constructed (and approved) charter and covers
three primary areas:

1. *Enablement governance* provides the mechanism for making
   strategic decisions, resolving conflicts and staying connected
   to senior leadership's vision for the company.
2. *Enablement production* includes all of the steps from the
   design of an enablement service through creation, localization, deployment, and the adoption and reinforcement of
   services.
3. *Enablement analytics* addresses how you will measure success.
   This includes metrics that measure the impact of enablement
   activities and services on various key performance indicators
   as well as how well enablement functions as a cross-functional
   team.

In this chapter, we'll take a closer look at enablement governance and production. Then, in Chapter 12, we'll tackle enablement metrics.

Enablement Governance

Your enablement governance model is designed to help you engage executive sponsors, stay connected to the organization's strategies and objectives and solve strategic issues. It also provides the mechanisms through which you report on the progress of your initiatives and their impact on the business. With an effective enablement governance model, enablement rises from a tactical function to a strategic discipline. Without it, enablement will always be fighting for the support and resources it needs.

> With an effective enablement governance model, enablement rises from a tactical function to a strategic discipline. Without it, enablement will always be fighting for the support and resources it needs.

You laid the foundation for enablement governance when you engaged senior executives in the review and approval of your charter. Now you need to keep them engaged. One of the best ways we've found of doing that is through an *enablement advisory board*.

To be clear, your enablement advisory board serves a different purpose than the collaboration model we talked about in Chapter 9. Collaboration is tactical in nature and the individuals involved are those you work with every day in the processes of creating and delivering effective enablement services. In contrast, your enablement advisory board is strategic in nature and consists of senior executives who are more focused on results than on the micro-details of how you achieve them.

Here are a few pointers for setting up your advisory board:

Establish a clear purpose. In meetings, members of the board can learn more about what enablement is doing and how it is impacting the business. Visibility into enablement will allow the advisory board members to provide input on strategic direction, ensuring enablement stays aligned to the company objectives and strategies. Make this purpose clear to all members so they understand why they are devoting valuable time to these meetings. If they see the value, they are more likely to prioritize their involvement.

Communicate responsibilities. The primary responsibilities of the team should be:

- Defining and evolving the long-term sales force enablement strategy, ensuring that it is derived from the business strategy and supporting the sales strategy.
- Making strategic decisions that require a broad senior executive involvement.
- Solving conflicts that are too complex to be resolved by referencing the charter and collaboration model.

Focus on senior executives. This advisory board is making high-level decisions, so it's vital to have members with a strategic and long-term orientation. Inviting them to a meeting where more tactical members get immersed in details is a waste of their time. Executive leadership will also want to see the results of their enablement investments, and department heads will want to understand how their people are contributing, so be sure to report on any milestones or metrics that show your progress.

Establish a regular cadence. This might be quarterly or even monthly. Your cadence should be based on the dynamics of your business, but no matter how frequently you meet, make sure it is regular. This will establish a habit of meeting and help ensure it doesn't fall off in favor of other priorities.

Table 11.1 How to Set Up an Executive Advisory Board

Who	• 5–10 members (more than 10 encourages people to skip meetings). • Senior executive leaders who can make decisions, remove hurdles and commit resources. • Representatives from: Marketing, Sales Leadership (may need multiple depending on organization structure), Sales Operations, Product Development, Learning & Development, Human Resources, IT, Customer Experience and Service. • Ensure that the majority of these roles have a strategic, long-term perspective.
When	• Meet regularly, depending on your enablement state and progress. Often, a quarterly rhythm works best (meeting format depends on culture). • Strive for an in-person meeting once annually if possible (coincide with sales kickoff, for example).
Tips	• Keep to a very tight agenda: Initiatives underway, results achieved against charter, actions needed to progress, upcoming initiatives, call for feedback, process through decisions to be made. • Use first meeting to officially approve your enablement charter. • Send out prereads with additional detail. • Plan for formal reporting of results at minimum quarterly.

Table 11.1 outlines how to create and use an enablement advisory board.

A Formal Governance Model Helps Answer the Tough Questions

There will be many situations where having a formal governance model can help keep your enablement efforts on track and collaboration running smoothly. Conflicts across functions can reach a point where the collaboration model and your charter might not be enough. For example, you might acquire a company that sells through a different channel, such as a network of independent resellers. A scenario like this will require some strategic decisions to be made: Do you provide enablement services to this new channel? If so, do the services need to be tailored to that audience, or do you treat them just as you would your internal sales teams? Who from the channel organization needs to be involved in their enablement, and what contributions will they make to the effort?

No doubt, it's likely there will also be conflicts between teams and functions as you sort these questions out. This is especially true if the acquired organization has a different philosophy on enablement and what their channel partners need. Your governance model, especially your advisory board, can be extremely helpful in arriving at an effective approach that supports your charter and the organization's goals—but doesn't leave both sides at each other's throats.

Enablement Production

Enablement production includes all of the steps from the design of an enablement service through creation, localization, deployment, analytics and the adoption and reinforcement of services (see Figure 11.2). Enablement isn't responsible for performing all of these steps, but it is accountable for ensuring they are carried out as effectively and efficiently as possible. Again, the orchestrating role is mission critical.

> *Define and Map.* In addition to defining the structure of the service (what it should look like), enablement also needs to define the purpose of the service (why it is necessary), the target audience (internal/external), which phase(s) of the customer's path it addresses, whether verticalization or localization will be required, the anticipated impact and

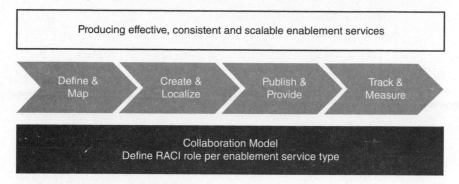

Figure 11.2 The Sales Force Enablement Production Process

how that impact will be measured. If it is designed to be a customer-facing service, such as a customizable presentation, enablement must also define the targeted buyer role, the relevant phase of the customer's path and business challenges.

Create and Localize. This step covers all the activities that are necessary to create the services as you've defined them. Your collaboration model should click into high gear as you orchestrate the efforts from many contributors. Remember to provide for localization of services as well. Many organizations create content and training services that are "ready to be localized," so that regional teams can use their understanding of the language and customs to help them resonate better with the target audience.

To execute this process step well, you need to have your value messages in place (refer back to Chapter 8). If you are running a value messaging project in parallel to creating services, you will need the results now, or you will need to plan to go back and revise services once messaging is complete and approved.

Publish and Provide. It's not enough to create services. You also need to make them easily accessible. Content needs to be easy to find, ideally through a system, such as CRM, that sales is comfortable using. It should also be searchable (or automatically generated) based on opportunity criteria and the customer's path phase. For training, all different training modalities must be considered: classroom, web-based, hybrid, eLearning and mLearning (mobile learning) as well as on-demand refresher training services to support current opportunities. Just as with content services, training services need to be made easily accessible.

Track and Measure. All types of enablement services need to be tracked and measured. We'll get into enablement metrics, including what to measure and how to set expectations in your charter, in greater detail in Chapter 12.

An Enablement Leader's Perspective

In a recent interview, Thierry van Herwijnen, a long-time enablement leader and host of The Sales Enablement Lab provided his perspectives on the enablement production process.

Define and Map

"When you define enablement services, identify what is required. This can either be part of new campaigns, in the case of a launch or part of a governance process like an annual content review cycle. The easiest way is to standardize this. Sales teams love consistency so try to develop a standard so sellers know what to expect. Check the relevance to the campaign. Sometimes all content types are required but sometimes a content type does not make sense. Like a case of a client success story for a product which has never been sold yet."

Value Messaging as Part of "Create and Localize"

"This is typically the hardest part. Especially for a product, solution or service across multiple business units. Get the key stakeholders in the room and develop a joint vision and value proposition. Agree on: who are the buyers, what business problem do they try to address, why does the current approach not work, what do we have to offer to address the business problem, how is our product/solution/service different compared to the competition, what is the risk if the customer does not change its approach, what will be the expected business outcome the customer will see by implementing our product/service/solution, what proof points do we have to show?

"After developing the value proposition it is time to do a deeper dive and interview the subject matter experts. This might be your key stakeholders but typically this is another group of deep experts. Based on what you have in your writing templates, ask deep open-ended questions to start building your content."

Create and Localize

"Then write your content. Use the value proposition as your strategy and guidance combined with the deep knowledge of the subject matter experts. Then review all the content with your key stakeholders and the subject matter experts. Make adjustments where necessary."

Publish and Provide

"Make the content available to the sellers. After this put it under a strict governance process. Content typically gets inaccurate fast. The competition changes, the external environments changes, your own capabilities change. Review all your content at least every 6 to 12 months."

Avoiding Missteps

The biggest mistake we see in enablement production is when the team doesn't give one of these steps the attention it deserves. Here are some common examples:

- Not mapping services to the customer's path.
- Creating a service for a home geography with no provision for localizing it for other geographies.

- Being disconnected from the latest results from the value messaging initiative.
- Failing to consider how the services will be delivered, e.g., creating content, but then not addressing how sales will find and use the content they need.
- Collaborating on one step only, such as create and localize, but failing to collaborate on each of the other steps.
- Creating the services without defining how you will measure their effectiveness.
- Not leveraging the metrics gathered or anecdotal feedback to further refine services and identify gaps.

Governance and Production Aren't Enough

We live in a results-driven world. This is especially true for sales organizations and any roles that interact with sales. Unless your sales force enablement discipline can show results, there is no reason to expect the organization to continue to invest.

We'll devote the next chapter to metrics, what you should measure and why. We'll also talk about the need for sales force enablement leaders to set realistic expectations early and to tie those expectations and results to their enablement charter and their enablement maturity.

Questions to Consider

- What are some of the tough questions an enablement advisory board could help us answer?
- Which executives should be recruited for our enablement advisory board and why? How often should we meet?
- Which steps of the production process is our enablement team best at orchestrating, and which steps need improvement? What actions can we take to make those improvements?

- How can we ensure enablement has the cross-functional support it needs to effectively collaborate at each stage?

Immediate Actions

Jot down two to three immediate actions you can take to improve enablement operations.

12

Measuring Results

Key Points

- Sales enablement leaders must set appropriate expectations for results when they create their charter and manage expectations through the sales force enablement advisory board.
- The metrics you choose should be relevant to your stage of enablement maturity.
- Sales enablement professionals should use a balance of objective versus subjective metrics and leading versus lagging indicators to paint a clear picture.

How Do We Know if We Are Successful?

It's a difficult question to answer. Not the least of our problems is the fact that sales force enablement is multifaceted with a lot of variables impacting results—not all of which are definable or under our control. Beyond that, our selling methodology, the customer's perspectives and buying processes, and the markets we are operating in are all very complex with many different but interrelated dimensions. Identifying a simple cause and effect relationship between an activity and a result is challenging if not impossible. If you don't consider all the variables, it's easy to misinterpret your data.

Yet, measuring the impact of enablement investments is an important and necessary step because it connects your efforts to your enablement charter and the objectives of the organization. It also allows you to report on your contribution to the success of the business to the senior executives on your enablement advisory board. At the end of the day, the measured impact supports your business case or it doesn't. It can either underline the purpose of your enablement practice or not.

Nevertheless, less is more. It doesn't make a lot of sense to measure everything just because you can. Focus on those metrics that you can impact with enablement services. Based on that, we can't emphasize enough the importance of setting expectations appropriately. Nothing damages your credibility more than making promises you can't deliver. Nothing will do more to ensure you don't get the necessary support or funding.

In this chapter, we're going to talk about how to measure enablement success, which metrics to use at various stages of enablement maturity and the importance of setting expectations early.

It Isn't All About Revenue

Before we jump into how you should measure success, we want to discuss a common misconception. In enablement discussions, online and with clients, we hear the same refrain over and over: "Enablement is all about revenue."

Revenue is important. For most C-level executives, it is the metric they care about most. It's the top line of the company, the one metric that keeps the company in business, and if yours is a public company, the metric that keeps the stock prices climbing. In our enablement research, increasing revenues is the top performance goal year after year, a strong indication that senior management expects enablement to have a positive impact.

"Sales enablement is a strategic business case related to capabilities, not directly to numbers, but to achieve the desired numbers."

Robert Racine, Sales Enablement Leader

However, as enablement professionals, we need to take a step back and ask: "If an increase in revenue is what we're looking for, how do we get there?" From an enablement perspective, jumping to revenue as the only metric that matters keeps us from seeing how what we do influences revenue. It's vital to consider the question of metrics from this angle before getting into any discussion of which metrics are the right ones to track.

We also need to be clear on one very important point: There is no direct causation between enablement efforts and revenue. There are only correlations. That's why, in this chapter, we're not going to talk specifically about overarching goals like increasing revenue. Instead, we'll discuss how to measure your progress to get to the expected topline results such as revenue. We're going to look at the question of metrics pragmatically so that you can ultimately influence the performance metrics that are discussed in the boardroom.

Success Is Tied to Maturity

Way back in Part One, we introduced four different levels of enablement maturity: random, organized, scalable and adaptive (see Figure 12.1). How you define success and the metrics you use to measure success need to be appropriate to the maturity of your enablement discipline.

As you move from a random approach to one that is organized, success is about the milestones and KPIs that show progress.

In this early stage, change is the order of the day as you define a new approach, and perhaps, implement new technology. It is

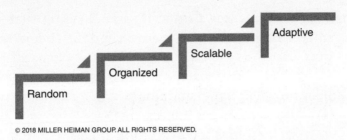

Figure 12.1 The Sales Force Enablement Maturity Model

still too early to expect, let alone measure, any impact on sales productivity or performance. Instead, success should be measured in milestones that show the progress of your initial efforts.

Enablement organizations at this stage often have limited resources as they're still trying to prove themselves, so they may focus more heavily on one area, such as training, to the exclusion of others. In this case, the milestones and KPIs you choose should be related to your area of focus.

Best Practice: Leverage Metrics Mechanisms Already in Place

It is likely that your collaboration partners will have some mechanisms already in place to measure the impact of what they do. The data they collect may be sufficient, or by collaborating you may be able to collect even deeper data by enhancing the methods used.

As an example, learning and development often used the Kirkpatrick-Philips model, which covers five levels of data collection.

> *Level 1: Reaction and Planned Action.* Usually a survey is issued immediately following the training. This determines whether salespeople and managers were prepared for their participation in a learning intervention, collects their reaction to the learning experience and their immediate plans for how they will apply learnings.

Level 2: Learning and Confidence. Evaluates what degree of learning has taken place, often in the form of a quiz. Answers the questions: Do sales managers and salespeople recall the content accurately? Are they confident in their understanding?

Level 3: Application and Implementation. This is collected at a set period after a training milestone (for example, 30 days post-training). Here, data is collected that evaluates whether new behaviors and knowledge have transferred back to the job and are being demonstrated by sellers and their managers in selling activities.

Level 4: Business Impact. This connects behavior change, skills use, methodology use, product knowledge and other learning outcomes to leading indicator business results such as conversion rates, sales cycle length, pipeline volume and customer scores. It answers the questions: Are attendees who demonstrate they have learned the material actually doing better? Is the training service impacting the leading indicators?

Level 5: Return on Investment. An intensive measurement project, Level 5 evaluation is generally reserved for only the highest risk or highest visibility interventions. Here the team quantifies the full ROI of a learning investment including tangible and monetized intangible benefits (isolating training from other variables that drive financial results) in comparison to burdened costs.

As enablement becomes scalable, productivity improvements should start to be measurable.

Enablement scalability is about doing more with less. As you progress to this level, you should be able to measure productivity improvements both in your enablement efforts and in your sales team.

In sales, productivity metrics describe an improved relationship between input and output. It's about doing things right and doing them more efficiently than before. The CSO *Insights 2017*

World Class Sales Practices Study shows that salespeople are spending less than 30% of their time selling. Services that help sales professionals find more time to sell are a great place to focus at this level.

Relevant KPIs for content services at this stage might be focused on a reduction in the time salespeople spend searching for content, a reduction in the time salespeople spend creating their own content and an improved collaboration between marketing and sales enablement that reduces the time it takes to produce a piece of content.

"It's our responsibility to ensure that our salespeople are hitting their targets so that the company can achieve the revenue targets. One of our key performance indicators to achieve this goal is onboarding ramp-up time, which we are constantly trying to shorten. From the first day you get started as a sales rep, we provide you with the right training, with the right content and value messaging, with everything you need to know so that you can be successful here at CallidusCloud."

Christine Dorrion, VP Global Sales & Channel Operations and Enablement, CallidusCloud

---

Another example, and the second-highest productivity goal in the study, is reduced ramp-up time for newly hired salespeople. In the 2016 Sales Performance Optimization Study, 39% of sales leaders said it took 10 months or more to bring new hires to full productivity. In fact, it took more than a year in 18% of organizations. An improvement of even a month or two can translate into a substantial improvement in results. Sales force enablement can have an impact by creating onboarding enablement programs that consist of content and training services specifically geared toward bringing the new hire up to speed as fast as possible.

In an adaptive enablement organization, productivity improvements lead to performance results (see Figure 12.2).

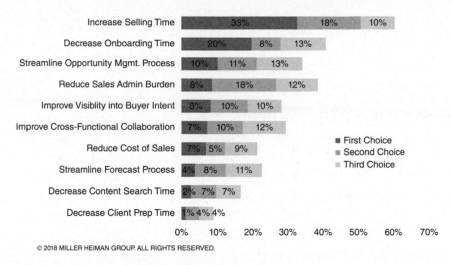

Figure 12.2 Top Sales Productivity Goals

Once you've improved productivity, you have a chance to improve performance. So, now it's time to start measuring the impact of your efforts on performance goals. Examples of those KPIs include increased revenues, increased win rates, decreased loss rates, decreased no-decision rates, increased margins and so on. Which ones you choose to focus on should be determined by which metrics are most important to the organization. At this stage, it's okay to focus on revenues, but don't forget to include the other KPIs that are tied to the organization's goals.

Managing Expectations

Now that you've decided how you will measure success, you need to share that with relevant stakeholders so that you can keep their expectations realistic. This clarity begins when you create your enablement charter. You should review these expectations each time you meet with your sales enablement advisory board and review your results. This is essential for two reasons. First, executive leadership will be impatient for real results, and you need to remind them of the charter, including the integrated roadmap, to which they agreed. Second, you need to show that you are living up to your end of the agreement by sharing your progress. The

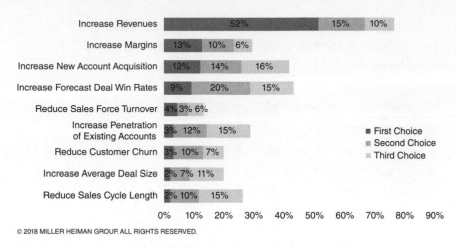

Figure 12.3 Top Sales Performance Goals

top sales performance goals from the 2017 study are shown in Figure 12.3.

When managing expectations, it's also important to keep in mind that there will be a natural time lag between the introduction of an enablement service and its impact on performance. For example, if you introduce a new sales methodology and new value messaging training along with related, updated sales content, the lag time between training and results is going to be at least as long as the average sales cycle. If it's not unusual for opportunities to remain in the funnel for six months or more in your organization, you're probably not going to see any impact for the first couple of quarters. It might even be longer as it can take time for salespeople to assimilate and apply what they've learned and for their sales managers to learn to coach them effectively.

Subjective Versus Objective Metrics

When setting metrics for enablement services, it helps to remember Albert Einstein's advice, "Not everything that can be counted counts, and not everything that counts can be counted."

With the rapid advancements in computing power and applications, it seems we can measure almost anything. Objective measurements such as conversion rates by stage, win rates, average deal size, sales cycle length and average account billing are increasingly easy to gather from sales and enablement technologies. However, success also needs to be measured by the things we can't count.

> "Not everything that can be counted counts, and not everything that counts can be counted."
>
> Albert Einstein

You are going to have to rely on subjective input and anecdotal evidence at least some of the time. This type of subjective tracking and measuring relies on feedback and observed evidence. How useful do sales professionals say the services you provide are? Which ones do they say they rely on most and when do they use them? What do they like? How do they think they could be made better? What do their prospects and customers think about the ones they use? See Table 12.1 for examples of objective and subjective metrics.

For example, analyzing the value of internal enablement content, such as a playbook, is more difficult because metrics like downloads, clicks or views say nothing about the content's value and impact. These metrics may be interesting, but they may also be irrelevant and not worth the effort of tracking. Only by talking with the members of your sales force and listening to their feedback can you understand how the asset is being used and to what effect. Understanding how your prospects and customers use the content your salespeople share with them is essential to making better content decisions and providing guidance on how and when to use specific types of content.

A word of caution when gathering anecdotal feedback. Unless your service is particularly good or bad, most people will be lukewarm on their feedback. Even then, there will be those who are reluctant to criticize because they don't want to be viewed as negative or reluctant to praise because that just isn't their style. If you

Table 12.1   Example Metrics

Objective Metrics		
Activity	**Productivity**	**Performance**
• Achievement of milestones within the roadmap • Utilization of services (lagging) • Reduced search time for content (leading)	• Conversion rates by stage (leading) • Time looking for content (leading) • Selling time (leading) • Ramp-up time (leading) • Sales cycle length (lagging) • Quality of meetings (customer survey)	• Win rates of forecasted deals (lagging) • Average deal size (lagging)

Subjective Metrics		
Activity	**Productivity**	**Performance**
• Anecdotal feedback from stakeholders on executive advisory board	• Anecdotal feedback from frontline sellers and sales managers	• Success case stories from sellers linking enablement, performance and results • Qualitative voice of customer data • Win/loss qualitative data

gather feedback from everyone and try to analyze it, at best, you'll get an average view that does little to help you know where you need to improve.

A better approach is to single out the extremes and look for patterns. For example, target the very low adopters of services and the very high adopters and gather their feedback. Your very low adopters might have certain work styles that make your services hard to access. Conversely, your very high adopters might be personality types that value learning more in general and are willing to put more effort into accessing and using services.

You should also factor in the performance levels of the salespeople. What services do high performers use most and what services do they think need work? How do they use these services in their role? While you need to ensure your enablement efforts are designed to bring everyone up to their full potential, these interviews with the high performers can give you a better idea of what works even if the evidence is anecdotal.

Finally, gather feedback from your customers as well. How would they describe their relationship with your sales team? Do they see your organization as anything more than a preferred supplier? How could the sales team add more value to your customers' organizations?

Leading Indicators: Your Early Warning System

Revenue. Bookings. Win/loss rates. No matter how your organization measures sales results, these metrics share a common trait: They measure the past, and *by the time you can measure sales results, it's too late to do anything about them.*

> By the time you can measure sales results, it's too late to do anything about them.

Way too many sales organizations are focused on past performance. This focus may work for sales leaders, but it's not the right approach for sales managers, especially those at the frontline, who are expected to impact and improve results. And it's certainly not the right approach for sales enablement leaders who are developing services designed to build capabilities that impact performance further down the road.

In an ever-changing sales environment, sales enablement leaders and sales managers need to be able to read the signals that tell them what sort of results they can expect, sometimes months before they happen. They also need an early warning system that can let them know when they're getting off track. Metrics called leading indicators can help.

Conversion rates are a good example of a leading indicator that can help predict future performance. Conversion rates can be used to measure the rate at which leads convert to opportunities. They can also be used to measure conversions for different lead and opportunity stages.

Leading indicators can often be measured in a number of ways, giving you the flexibility to tailor your metrics to the needs and goals of the organization. For example, conversion rates can be measured by volume, value or velocity.

- Volume: The number of leads that turned into an opportunity in a given time frame.
- Value: The financial value of the leads that turned into an opportunity, in a given time frame, measured in your currency.
- Velocity: How fast leads are converted into opportunities, typically measured in units of time such as days or weeks.

No matter how you decide to measure conversion rates, higher conversion rates at each stage of the selling process should lead to future increases in sales and revenues.

Here are a few more examples of leading indicators to consider:

- Ratio of first contact to follow-up meetings.
- Number of contact attempts required.
- Ratio of marketing-qualified leads to sales-accepted leads.
- Email response rates.
- Open rates for content shared with prospects and customers.
- Conversion rates between phases of the customer's journey.
- Seller competencies as assessed by sales leaders.

When deciding which leading indicators to track, remember to pick indicators appropriate for your enablement maturity level. As we said when we began our discussion on metrics, you will probably have relatively few of them in the early stages when you're just trying to get your discipline organized. At that stage, you're more focused on milestones than metrics. As your discipline matures, you will start tracking more leading indicators, such as conversion rates, that are directly related to results. A mature enablement discipline is one that knows, through objective measurements, which leading indicators lead to results.

Final Words of Advice on Setting Metrics

To avoid paralysis by analysis at every stage of enablement maturity, you should limit your measurements to a handful and be specific about what you are measuring and why. Remember, you will be reporting on these to your advisory board, so make sure they are meaningful, appropriate to your maturity stage, and that you can measure them without too much wasted effort.

As with any metrics, visibility is important and role-specific dashboards can help sales enablement leaders stay on top of the impact of their enablement services, especially as they pilot new approaches. For example, imagine you are piloting new value messaging with the sales team. You will be working alongside the sales managers, evaluating how well sales professionals understand the value messages and can deliver them in the field. You'll be looking at what other services are needed, such as revisions to the value messaging, additional related coaching services, or additional training. A dashboard that tracks conversion rates can give you an early indication of what's working and what isn't and save you from having to wait a full sales cycle before adjusting your approach.

Collaborate with your colleagues in sales operations to ensure that your targeted audiences, such as sales managers, get their own dashboards with those early indicators that can help them manage performance. Remember, it's fine for sales leaders to look at past results, but sales managers on the frontline need indicators of what those results will be while there's still time to improve them.

Finally, remember that you need to build your enablement discipline on a foundation of realistic expectations. The impact of your enablement efforts will be more long-term than short-term, and how you measure results will vary at each stage of development. Setting expectations starts at the beginning with your charter and continues every time you meet with your advisory board.

"We believe that it is difficult to isolate the impact of individual initiatives and that, rather, it is a combination of factors that drives improvement in results. For example, you can build a team of the best reps based on their Predictive Index profiles, however, if you have unskilled managers supporting those reps, then you are not going to get the maximum leverage.

"Consequently, we look to what I would describe as 'macro' indicators. The first, and highest order key performance indicator, is productivity improvement. By way of example, in our Caribbean region, which is our largest in terms of revenue, number of countries and number of sales professionals, and where we have arguably seen the biggest adoption of our sales enablement efforts, the output per rep increased 37% in the first half of 2017 versus the first half of 2016. And this is roughly the same order of magnitude increase in productivity from 2015 to 2016. Again, we cannot ascribe this incredible performance improvement to a single initiative—or allocate the impact among initiatives—but we are confident that the portfolio of enablement programs working in concert have led to this improvement.

"There are, of course, a host of other metrics we monitor that are leading, leaning or lagging indicators of the impact our sales enablement efforts have on results.

And all of them are trending positively when compared with the prior year: Average deal size continues to grow and speaks to the ability of our sales reps to more effectively position and sell holistic solutions versus just products; forecast accuracy continues to improve, leading to more predictable and consistent sales production; number of reps meeting or exceeding quota continues to steadily increase meaning we rely less on a few top performers to deliver overall results; win rates continue to improve, which indicates that we are qualifying opportunities better and managing sales cycles more effectively.

"While all of these metrics and reports are consumed and acted on by the sales leadership in each market, we now disseminate high-level sales KPI reports to the executive leadership team. Furthermore, the overall sales results are reviewed at least quarterly as part of a corporate commercial review that is conducted with our executive leadership team up to and including our CEO."

Boris Kluck, VP Sales Operations,
Cable & Wireless Communications

Questions to Consider

- How do we define success, and how do we measure it? Are the metrics we use appropriate to our enablement maturity level?
- How can we create a better balance between subjective/objective and leading/lagging metrics?
- What metrics should we be measuring that we aren't today?
- Have we set expectations properly with key stakeholders and our executive leadership?

Immediate Actions

Jot down the two or three leading indicators that would be appropriate to measure at your current state of enablement maturity.

PART

V

Where to Go from Here

PART FIVE LANDS the plane, so to speak. Here we give direction on where to take your sales enablement journey next and the urgency for doing so in the near-term.

In Chapter 13, we distill our discussions on enablement into a comprehensive maturity model. The purpose of this framework is to help you take a step back and look at your sales enablement discipline holistically. Where are you today and where would you like to be? This provides guidance on specifically where to begin your next phase of enablement. In the previous chapters, we've outlined dozens upon dozens of potential actions to take. However, it is a practical impossibility to take them all. Chapter 13 helps you make the hard decisions on your priorities.

Chapter 14 puts an eye to the future as a source of urgency for taking action. As fast as your customers are changing today, that is only a glimpse of what is to come. Drastic changes are anticipated in buy-sell cycles, the roles of customer-facing personnel and the profile for who will be successful in sales. The impact of those changes is broad reaching and sales enablement, as orchestrator, is in the unique position of being able to coordinate a response. However, the future in this context isn't that far away. Sales enablement will need to take the lead in exploring these future realities today.

13

Enablement Maturity: Where Are You Now and How Can You Evolve Your Practice?

Key Points

- Evolving sales enablement maturity requires a candid assessment of where you are today.
- Enablement is, and should be, different in each organization. Your business context will help you determine what maturity level you should target for enablement maturity.
- Advancing sales enablement maturity requires a methodical approach for incrementally shoring up gaps in the clarity model.

AT THIS POINT in the book, you have hopefully learned a lot about enablement and begun to consider your specific situation. Now it is time to pull it all together into a go-forward approach. In this chapter, we provide a maturity model that will help you to assess the current enablement maturity in your organization and focus your actions.

Before we get into the specifics of the model, there are two things that will be helpful in making decisions based on your maturity assessment:

1. *Estimating your current point of departure is essential.* You can only define your journey into the future if you have a very clear view of where you are right now. Be very candid in your assessment. There is no right or wrong current state. There is just YOUR current state. And that's all that matters. When looked at holistically, World-Class sales enablement is a very tall order. And all organizations start at the lowest level of maturity ... not having a sales enablement discipline at all. At the same time, you may have been working at your sales enablement journey for some time, and it is important that you show the fruits of your efforts. However, you should resist the temptation to exaggerate your progress. Sometimes the best learnings come from understanding what hasn't worked. There is always something to be improved. The most important thing at the beginning of your enablement journey is to accept where you are.

2. *When putting a stake in the ground on where you want to be, consider that your ideal maturity level is not always the most advanced maturity level.* Instead, your ideal enablement maturity level depends on your organization's context. An organization that provides highly commoditized products that are primarily sold online may choose to target service professionals for enablement as they have the greatest influence on renewal business. The segment of the customer's path that anchors enablement will be the implementation phase and an informal discipline may be all that is required. On the other hand, an organization with highly complex service offerings and long sales cycles that has a high dependence on bringing in new logos will need at least a formal enablement maturity in order to connect marketing and sales, align content to the customer's

path, etc. Every organization will have very different enablement approaches and may well have a different ideal state.

> When putting a stake in the ground on where you want to be, consider that your ideal maturity level is not always the most advanced maturity level. Instead, your ideal enablement maturity level depends on your organization's context.

The maturity model, then, does not act as recognition for, or an indictment of, your efforts. It should be used simply as a way to prioritize your actions going forward. As we have discussed extensively in this text, there are a limitless number of initiatives that can be orchestrated under the umbrella of sales enablement. No one has a limitless budget though. So, prioritization and focus will always be necessary.

In alignment with the other maturity models discussed in this book, the overarching enablement maturity model is structured with four levels of maturity: Random, Organized, Scalable and Adaptive (see Figure 13.1). For each level, we provide a description of the clarity model so that you may place your function into one level or another. As you read the following descriptions, consider which best describes your enablement discipline.

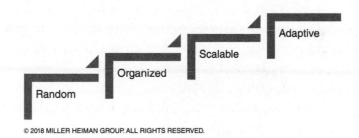

Figure 13.1 The Sales Force Enablement Maturity Model

Random: Enablement Does Not yet Exist

This maturity level describes the level where most organizations begin. They have a training program or a content initiative and want to grow it into a full-fledged enablement discipline. When at the start of your enablement journey, you will find that the facets of your clarity model can be described as follows:

Customer as design point. There is not yet a defined design point as to how enablement should be designed. It is born of the initiatives versus being born of the customer path.

Strategy, charter and sponsorship. Initiatives are led in an ad hoc manner to react to productivity or performance challenges and led in a project mode. There is no executive sponsorship beyond departmental levels. A charter is not in place, and an enablement strategy is missing. Enablement is perceived as a tactical weapon to fix an operational problem.

Audience of customer-facing roles and their managers. There is no formal definition of any target audiences beyond what is identified on a project-by-project basis, e.g., buying a negotiations program for strategic account managers.

Enablement services. Various enablement services are created by various departments and are not in alignment with each other. These are often pushed to the sales force by throwing services over the fence versus via an integrated and holistic implementation approach.

Formalized collaboration. There is no formal approach to cross-functional collaboration. Collaboration, if needed, is based on ad hoc approaches only: "Someone call Marketing to be sure we have the latest collateral referenced in the role play that is due today."

Integrated technology. Enablement technology is based on point solutions implemented by various departments, based on their perspective for how to help sales. As a result, sellers are asked to sign into and enter data into multiple systems, duplicating efforts and using manual processes.

Enablement operations. This enablement backbone does not exist in a random approach. Every project involves reinventing the wheel.

Organized: Enablement Exists but in a Narrow Fashion

This maturity level shows a lot more structure than the random approach. Here initiatives are linked together by a common view and a practical understanding of the scope of enablement. However, this is often confined to one department or function. And usually, services begin with one domain (content or training) and work on putting the infrastructure in place to expand the scope and impact of such services.

Customer as design point. Customers are considered the center of attention. However, the internal marketing, sales and service process landscape is designed from the inside to the outside, often very product-driven rather than customer-challenge driven.

Strategy, charter and sponsorship. An informal vision of sales enablement is available, but it is not as detailed as a formal charter. Enablement is usually supported by one executive sponsor rather than having the support of cross-functional executive sponsorship. The approach may be confined to a single department or business unit.

Audience of customer-facing roles and their managers. The audience is usually exclusively salespeople.

Enablement services. Those in the organized level of maturity focus on one area to begin with such as training or content. However, unlike random maturity, this level of enablement maturity looks at how to ensure alignment and consistency of services within that services area. For example, bringing all training together into one integrated curricula or all content together into one body of knowledge.

Formalized collaboration. Cross-functional collaboration does occur more deliberately at this level. It is based on an informal approach that defines a set of ideas for how to work together one project or one initiative at a time.

Integrated technology. This maturity level is still focused on point solutions. However, these solutions are approached from the departmental perspective rather than from the salespeople's perspective. This maturity level also focuses more on access in the workflow, providing mobile access per point solution as needed.

Enablement operations. Enablement operations as defined earlier does not exist in an informal approach. However, there might be some repeatable processes in place. For example, there may be a standard way for conducting product launches.

Scalable: Enablement Becomes Holistic, Aligned and Integrated

This maturity level takes enablement to the next level, from a single structured domain to an integrated approach that covers all enablement services and also ensures that the primary design point is the customer's path.

Customers. The customer's path is the main design point. The existing internal processes from marketing to sales to service are integrated and are formally aligned to the customer's path.

Strategy, charter and sponsorship. The vision has been formalized, based on a structured process of mapping the business strategy with the sales strategy and the current level of performance. Specific enablement goals are defined and relevant enablement services have been defined. A roadmap that describes how to get there has been developed. All of this detail is captured in a formal enablement charter, approved by all involved senior executive stakeholders.

Audience of customer-facing roles and their managers. The audience is salespeople *and* their managers. Sometimes, the audience also includes all customer-facing roles, such as service associates, which are handled from a sales perspective.

Enablement services. An enablement discipline at this maturity level provides integrated enablement services, aligned by a comprehensive value messaging approach. As sales managers are also a target audience, coaching services that consist of training, content and tools are also part of the enablement services portfolio.

Formalized collaboration. Collaboration partners and clear collaboration goals are defined and communicated. The accountable and responsible roles are defined for each enablement service, as well as the roles to be informed and consulted.

Integrated technology. At this maturity level, the CRM system is considered the anchor for all enablement technologies. Enablement content solutions, sales learning solutions as well as coaching tools are integrated in the CRM system to allow the target audiences a one-stop-shopping experience. This also supports increased adoption and data accuracy within the CRM.

Enablement operations. Enablement operations processes exist. Ideally, an advisory board and a clear governance protocol have been established to keep the senior executives engaged and to allow the charter to become a living foundation of the enablement discipline. Furthermore, an enablement production process has been set up that defines the sequence of activities that are necessary to provide enablement services from definition and design, to creation, localization, publishing and tracking. And, in this maturity level, a set of leading and lagging indicators for measuring progress and impact has been defined.

Adaptive: Enablement Becomes Dynamic and CX Focused

This maturity level takes enablement from a scalable to an adaptive level, from structured domains to an integrated approach that covers all enablement services and also ensures that the primary design point is a continuously refined view of the customer's path to create an outstanding customer experience (CX).

Customer as the design point. The customer's path is the main design point, as it is in the scalable maturity level. The difference in this level is that the internal processes are derived from the customer's path, not aligned to the customer's path. There is a continuous re-evaluation and refining that is done to keep services and infrastructure aligned to changes in customers, customer paths, customer feedback, etc. At the adaptive maturity level, the customer's path is leveraged to deliver an outstanding customer experience.

Strategy, charter and sponsorship. All the elements of the scalable level are present. In addition, there is a fully functioning advisory board consisting of high-level executives from a range of business units. In this level, enablement reports to a C-level role that has a long-term, strategic focus such as the CEO, the chief revenue officer or the chief customer experience officer.

Audience of customer-facing roles and their managers. The audience of enablement comprises all customer-facing roles from a customer-experience perspective including their managers. In this maturity level, the main purpose is to create an exceptional customer experience that leads to more revenue and the desired margins. Customer service, customer success and service manager roles receive the same level of focus as salespeople and sales managers.

Enablement services. All services from the scalable maturity level are included and aligned to unified value messaging. Adaptive maturity demonstrates a focus on the full customer's path, not just the buying phase. For example, a special focus is devoted to value confirmation messaging to be delivered by service personnel in the implementation phase in order to ensure renewals and expansion of existing accounts.

Formalized collaboration. Collaboration occurs as described in the scalable maturity level. The difference is that at the highest level of enablement maturity, there is a prestige associated with being part of the enablement cross-functional team that drives participation. Enablement leaders find that they are being asked by change enablers in various departments to be included in their work (versus selling others on the idea). Being part of the enablement expanded team is considered a career enhancing assignment for high potentials being groomed for promotion. The leadership team considers collaboration here as an adaptive approach and as an essential success factor to create the desired customer experience, not as a soft factor only.

Integrated technology. Solutions are integrated into the CRM system, as described in the scalable level. In addition, the organization is leveraging artificial intelligence to create more selling time for salespeople, provide coaching direction to managers and to guide selling efforts to actions that are predicted to create the most success.

Enablement operations. Operations are formalized as defined in the previous level. In addition, there is an enhanced focus on metrics that are not only leading indicators, but also derived from the customer's path and the customer experience goals. Enablement professionals at this level track to a dashboard. They are able to quantify enablement impact and translate it into monetary benefit from improved productivity or effectiveness, calculating clear ROI to expand the discipline. There are clear production processes that use rapid development and detailed feedback to scale up enablement into a discipline capable of efficiently orchestrating many initiatives at once, keeping them aligned and integrated.

Acting on Your Assessment

Importantly, it is unlikely that you will score yourself the same for each component of the clarity model. For example, you may find that your enablement technologies are well integrated into your CRM system, a marker of formal maturity. However, at the same time, you may find that collaboration is very informal in nature.

Consider generally which level best describes where you are. Then, look to shore up your gaps within that level. For example, if you are mostly in the formal range but have informal collaboration, make that a priority. Once you see consistency in a level, then you are ready to launch an effort to move into the next level.

Moving from one maturity level to another requires evolution not revolution. You'll note that the major differences between one level and the next have to do with the breadth and depth of services, the integration and alignment of those services and the formality of the infrastructure in place to create and deliver them. This means that change needs to be undertaken methodically. Throwing out new playbooks, training and coaching programs would add to the volume of activity, but may not be as helpful as first building a value messaging framework to align existing services and creating the foundation for future services.

In the example shown in Table 13.1, the enablement discipline is mostly at the informal level, with some areas of formal

Table 13.1   Example Maturity Assessment

	Random	Informal	Formal	Dynamic
Customer		X		
Audience			X	
Strategy, Charter, Sponsorship		X		
Enablement Services		X		
Collaboration		X		
Technology	X			
Operations	X			

work and some areas in random. The best approach for this organization is to try to shore up gaps in technology and operations first. Based on its business context, in this case a global professional services firm, it makes sense for this organization to then target formal maturity. As you move up the levels of maturity, a great place to start is to work on your charter. The thinking (and the collaboration) process involved in creating a charter will, by definition, help you advance all components of the clarity model.

Questions to Consider

- What level of maturity is my organization at?
- Who else should I get to assess our enablement maturity?
- What is a realistic goal for my enablement discipline? An aspirational goal?

Immediate Actions

Visit the sales enablement expert site located at https://www.millerheimangroup.com/salesenablementguidebook to download an assessment tool for assessing your own maturity in more detail.

14

The Future of Selling Starts Now

Key Points

- Sales force enablement will be vital to helping sales organizations rapidly adapt to drastic changes expected in the buy-sell cycle, the role of customer-facing professionals and the profile of a successful salesperson.
- While framed in the context of the future, such changes need to be planned for today. AI learns and adapts. This means change will come much faster than the decade(s) it took for CRM adoption.
- Due to its role as orchestrator, sales enablement is in a unique position to help the sales organization not just prepare for the future challenges, but to take advantage of new opportunities.

Enabling the Future

Thus far, we've outlined what could potentially be a lot of work for your organization. As you get set to begin, or expand, your sales enablement journey, it's worth taking a glimpse into the future. Sales is changing rapidly, fueled by accelerating advances in technology and exponentially increasing demands from customers. What you sell, who you sell it to and how you sell it (and even who sells it) will all undergo massive redesign. With such significant changes to the very foundation of what we mean by selling, there are those who wonder whether sales enablement will be an integral part of selling organizations of the future or whether it is simply a temporary fix, used to facilitate a period of transition.

We argue that sales enablement is assuredly here to stay and will become even more important as the future becomes the present. Sales enablement *is* your path into the future.

Inevitable Changes That Sales Enablement Can Help You Prepare for Now

While no one can predict the future with certainty, there are changes well under way that can only be expected to continue.

The Buy/Sell Cycle Will Be Guided by AI

We talked about artificial intelligence briefly in our discussion on sales enablement technologies. In addition to AI changing how we sell, it will drastically change how buyers buy. Buyers will leverage AI-based technologies to learn about the solutions they buy and the suppliers they buy them from. There are new start-up organizations today that are banding together buyer data on their suppliers and applying AI technologies in order to calculate ideal price points, predict seller behavior and optimize the buying process. If sellers feel that they are behind the curve when it comes to buyer information now, it is only going to get worse once all their pricing models and selling processes become fully transparent.

On the flip side, sales organizations will continue to advance their use of AI as well. But be warned, if you can't stand the idea of your every move being analyzed, sales might be the wrong profession for you. In the future, sales professionals will be some of the most studied people on earth, with data gathering tools cap-turing everything they do and say as well as how prospects and customers respond.

For example, AI systems will use voice recognition capabili-ties to record sales calls and combine all that unstructured data with social media information, public domain information, pur-chasing data and more to proactively give guidance to the sales professional on what to do as well as when and how to do it. Such systems learn over time and reconfigure their algorithms to provide predictive insights and advice based on what is likely to be most successful. And it only grows stronger with data. Sys-tems will have the power to analyze millions of data points. Some developers are even talking about developing wearable biomet-rics devices that can gauge a sales professional's stress levels dur-ing a sales call.

AI-augmented enablement technology is like having a sales coach at the salesperson's side every moment of the workday, except these systems aren't guessing at what works or offering an often-flawed human perspective on how to approach the cus-tomer. AI will take the guesswork out of selling ... and out of buying.

> AI will take the guesswork out of selling ... and out of buying.

Sales, as a Job Function, Will Fundamentally Change

Since the buy-sell cycle is changing (the steps in the process, the time frames, the activities that take place), the role that the sales-person plays will be different, too.

One thing that will change (to much applause by sellers) is spending less time on the "tedium" of selling. Research shows that salespeople only spend about 35% of their time selling: connect-ing with buyers either in-person or in a virtual setting. The rest of the time is spent on a variety of tasks that, while important, don't do anything to add value for the customer. This includes tasks like filling out reports, traveling, attending training sessions, partici-pating in company meetings and a whole host of administrative tasks that must be done. AI will eliminate the need for, or greatly reduce the time spent, on these mundane activities. For example, no more entering meeting notes into the CRM system or trying to guess whether an opportunity will close. The same systems that automatically capture the salesperson's actions and words and the buyer's responses will transfer that data into the CRM system, giv-ing the salesperson more face time with customers.

But what to do with all that extra time? One response may be to reduce the number of sellers. And, some of that will happen within transactional selling models. However, another response within complex sales will be to refocus sellers on using the new guidance at their fingertips to creatively configure solutions, add value, become expert in the customer in order to increase deal size, increase lifetime value of customer, increase expansion and more.

The Future Is Already Here

William Gibson observed, "The future is already here, it is just not evenly distributed." A sales executive we interviewed, Kai Yu Hsiung, Silverline, www.silverlinecrm.com, showed us the advantage of being a first mover in the emerging AI-enabled sales space. Kai was part of the original Silverline team starting back in 2009. The company's vision was to be more than just another Salesforce consultancy. It wanted to innovate clients' businesses through combining consulting with robust indus-try accelerators, powerful AppExchange apps and leading-edge technology components.

Kai's role at Silverline has always been focused on revenue, starting initially as vice president of sales, then taking on the chief revenue officer role, and now serving as chief growth offi-cer. To achieve its growth goals, Silverline has not only focused on attracting the best talent in their ecosystem but also provid-ing those sales professionals with the best tools to optimize their performance. That objective motivated the company to be one of the early adopters of AI technology for sales.

In investigating sales solutions, Kai's team came across an AI-enabled system called Conversica. Kai told us, "We again did a pilot and started to uncover specific tasks that AI could perform to really benefit the sales organization. One of those was a new process to have Conversica take over many of the tasks related to customer renewals."

"In addition to the system integration work we do, we have a robust software as a service (SaaS) business as well. Today, we have over 5,000 customers utilizing hundreds of thousands of SaaS software licenses, and we have dedicated personnel to handle that renewal business. We are now re-engineering the process so that Conversica's platform will coordinate many of the renewal management tasks. If the renewal flows smoothly, Conversica will be able to handle everything through actual processing of the renewal order. This then frees up our personnel to focus on more complex renewals and perform more value-added tasks. That experiment is now under way to quantify what the total ROI is from decreasing the cost of the renewal process while at the same time increasing the renewal rate by 5 or 6%."

Kai shared that Silverline's experiences as an early adopter of AI for sales solutions has opened Silverline's eyes to the power of its emerging technology area and that it will be a game changer in the world of sales going forward.

This is the future of selling, more science than art. To be sure, the art is still there and the value of a human connection will still bring benefits to the right interactions in the right relationships. Yet such interactions will be guided and enhanced by science.

The Kind of Salespeople Who Will Be Successful Will Change

The future of selling will require professionals who are comfortable working with technology. They'll also need to be comfortable analyzing and relying on data to help them see a level deeper than what their eyes, their ears and their customers tell them. Back when selling was an art, organizations sought sellers who were "good with people" or demonstrated a high customer-orientation or emotional intelligence (EQ) score on hiring assessments. Today, we are seeing a shift from EQ to more analytical, systems thinking and technical skills. In fact, many organizations, including those not in the technology sector, are starting to look for individuals with more science-technology-engineering-mathematics (STEM) backgrounds, as their training helps make them better problem solvers in a technology- and data-rich environment. In fact, in a recent CSO Insights study investigating the growth of sales as a profession, STEM was the number two background for surveyed salespeople, behind only business degrees.

Sales Force Enablement Paves the Way to the Future

In reference to technology advancements, Bill Gates has said, "We always overestimate the change that will occur in the next 2 years, and underestimate the change that will occur in the next 10." We think that is true of AI, but the window of change may be more like 5 years than 10. Remember that AI learns and self-corrects and self-enhances. This means that AI will take hold substantially faster than CRM or other technologies that were often stymied by internal resistance to change, clunky first efforts and more.

> "We always overestimate the change that will occur in the next 2 years, and underestimate the change that will occur in the next 10."
>
> Bill Gates

If sales enablement is crucial now (and hopefully you've seen why over the course of this book), it will be absolutely vital moving forward. Sales enablement has the responsibility to help sales organizations get ready for and leverage these pending changes. Sales enablement understands the end goal of technology better than IT. Sales enablement professionals understand the sellers' needs better than marketing. They know what makes a successful seller better than HR. Sales leadership doesn't have the bandwidth to deeply investigate AI-augmented selling. They may be intrigued, but they're too busy worrying about next quarter's quota to do any sort of organized inquiry.

Sales enablement, in its role of orchestration across functions, is in a truly unique position to help organizations get ready for a quickly advancing future. Start today by establishing a mature, high-performing sales enablement discipline, while always looking for services (including AI-augmented technologies) that can be used to create a competitive advantage tomorrow.

In sales force enablement, the future starts now! Are you ready?

Questions to Consider

- How well prepared for the future is our sales organization?
- What signs are we seeing today that foreshadow changes to our selling model?
- Which executive(s) needs to get passionate about enablement to support our journey? And what business case must we build for them?

Immediate Actions

Do something! There is a myriad of ways to start or enhance your sales enablement efforts. But don't let the daunting nature of the scope of enablement stall your efforts. Start socializing it with executives today. Start the conversation!

Appendix

Sample Charter

ENABLEMENT CHARTER: *Example Co.*
REVISION DATE: *January 1, 20XX*
EXEC SPONSOR:
ENABLEMENT LEAD:
ADVISORY BOARD:

I. SITUATION

BUSINESS STRATEGY Key strategies, provide direction	■ Move from #2 to #1 position in enterprise market within 3 years, drive 10% CAGR ■ Leverage recent acquisitions in emerging markets to increase global business ■ Change model to more fee-based services, implement price increase ■ Reframe brand to be higher-end, higher touch as a differentiator
SALES STRATEGY Key elements of sales strategy, provide direction	■ Transform from a product-selling to a value-based selling approach ■ Aggressively pursue new logos through lead gen and prospecting

	■ Increase sales capacity by hiring 75 new sellers worldwide in next fiscal year ■ Create Global Account Management structure
REFERENCE DOCS Strategy docs to reference in conjunction with charter	■ Corporate strategy map, findings from annual business and sales reviews ■ Annual customer satisfaction survey results and recommendations ■ Brand strategy document ■ Enablement assessment findings report

II. WHAT SUCCESS LOOKS LIKE

VISION What will SE function do for the organization aspirationally?	Enablement will be the ultimate, enterprise-wide orchestrator across all departments that provide services to equip our customer-facing personnel. We will be accountable for delivering (directly or through others) *all* content, training, and coaching services and tools for *all* customer-facing sales and service roles, their managers and our channel. We will contribute to the achievement of our growth and customer experience targets by fundamentally changing the way that we sell to and serve our customers.
MISSION How will we get there?	Enablement will take a strategic and holistic approach, starting with existing services such as training and expanding rapidly into content and coaching, leveraging best-in-class operations, collaboration and technology to help our customer-facing associates be seen as strategic contributors and trusted partners by enhancing their ability to be valuable (Perspective Selling), relevant and differentiating for prospects and customers at all stages of the customer path, in every interaction.

OBJECTIVES Specifically, what will we achieve?	▪ Achieve all milestones as defined in the roadmap, on time, on budget ▪ Increase selling time (2 hours/salesperson in 18 months) by reducing search time and time spent on content creation ▪ Reduce ramp-up time from 24 weeks to 22 weeks ▪ Move from Preferred Vendor to Solutions Consultant on the SRP Matrix, measured by customer satisfaction scores of sellers on annual survey and win/loss reports ▪ Increase new logos in funnel by 10% ▪ Track win rates for forecasted deals to establish baseline (will set win rates goals as enablement function matures into World-Class phase from current required stage)
METRICS How do we measure success?	▪ Search time for content (hours/week) ▪ Time for content creation (hours/week) ▪ Additional selling time (hours/week) ▪ Ramp-up time to full productivity (weeks/salesperson) ▪ Relationship level (from preferred vendor to solutions consultant) based on customer survey ▪ New business with new accounts in pipeline ($/overall pipeline value) ▪ Conversion rates from lead to opportunity (value, volume, velocity) ▪ Win rate tracking (% of won opportunities, measured by their $ value) to establish win rate goal ▪ Quota attainment tracking to establish quota attainment goal

III. SCOPE OF ENABLEMENT

AUDIENCE Which roles, regions, etc. will be served?	<ul><li>Enterprise-wide</li><li>New hires to the sales and customer success organizations</li><li>Incumbent field, inside sales roles in all business units, including newly acquired businesses</li><li>Global account managers as defined in recent reorganization</li><li>Customer service roles that have been assigned upsell quotas</li><li>Frontline sales managers of roles above</li></ul>

IV. ROADMAP OF INITIATIVES AND SERVICES

BUILD SALES ENABLEMENT CAPABILITY	PROVIDE ENABLEMENT SERVICES
KICKOFF Q4, 2018	
Stand-up function <ul><li>Establish advisory board, formal collaboration network</li><li>Conduct audience needs analysis, mine existing data</li><li>Develop enablement master framework (diamond) to guide further activities</li></ul>	No services deployments during end of fiscal year. Use time to organize efforts and truly stand up the SE function

PHASE 1 Q1–Q2, 2019

Start by taking stock of training services (skills, methodology, process, technology, product, etc.) and fill immediate gaps

- Conduct full inventory of existing training services per role
- Eliminate redundant services and those that are no longer relevant
- Agree on curricula by role
- Create RACI chart and project plans for filling key gaps

Make formal commitment to roll out new training initiatives in conjunction with content and coaching

- Support hiring push, short-term urgency for 75 new hires
  - Partner with L&D, Marketing and Product Management to update onboarding with new brand, new market information
  - Partner with HR on sales mentoring program
  - Define and track productivity measures for new hires
  - Create new capabilities deck
- Roll out aligned services to support new GAM team
  - Partner with L&D to deploy Global Account Management methodology
  - Work with Sales Ops to launch tech-enabled account management tool
  - Provide managers with related coaching training and tools
  - Partner with marketing to provide data-based case studies, success stories and examples of global enterprise clients for use in awareness phase to establish shared visions of future success

PHASE 3 Q3–Q4 2019

Expand to connect content (customer-facing and internal) and training into an organized plan, mapped to the customer's path

- Map existing content assets to the customer's path
- Conduct content assessment in conjunction with Marketing, Product Management and representatives of your audiences and their customers
- Eliminate redundant assets and those that are no longer relevant
- Agree gaps to fill (start with content aligned to training curricula as it exists)

Begin to fill critical content gaps

- Build ROI tool and deploy with appropriate training and coaching support
- Conduct value messaging workshop based on value messaging framework
- Update related existing content assets, use new messaging for new assets
- Create customer-path-wide playbook for new markets, typical business issues and common buying scenarios
- Refresh outdated case studies and related assets

FUTURE

Expand audiences and scope to include managers and customer service.

Enhance services by improving Tech and Operations

- Select sales enablement content management platform
- Create metrics dashboard
- Define formal process for getting services to internal markets

- Expand services to include sales manager enablement program including a comprehensive coaching curricula, online tools and formalized coaching process
- Collaborate with marketing and sales leadership team to align both social strategies to ensure consistency along the customer's path
- Roll out social selling program that develops social selling skills and implements a new

	layer of content management that ensures current, shareable and social content to be shared on social networks, so that the target audiences can easily connect and engage with potential buyers ■ Roll out upsell/cross-sell program for appropriate service roles ■ Establish dynamic value messaging approach linked to new brand and markets and thread throughout all services covering the entire customer's path ■ Create a library of playbooks associated with key segments, paths that guide salespeople along the entire customer's path ■ Deploy SECM loaded with assessed, cleaned and improved up-to-date content and associated reinforcement and training services

Index